Performance and Rubrics for Early Elementary Mathematics

Performance tasks are highly effective tools to assist you in implementing rigorous standards. But how do you create, evaluate, and use such tools? In this bestselling book, educational experts Charlotte Danielson and Pia Hansen explain how to construct and apply performance tasks to gauge students' deeper understanding of mathematical concepts at the early elementary level. You'll learn how to:

◆ Evaluate the quality of performance tasks, whether you've written them yourself or found them online;
◆ Use performance tasks for instructional decision-making and to prepare students for summative assessments;
◆ Create your own performance tasks, or adapt pre-made tasks to best suit students' needs;
◆ Design and use scoring rubrics to evaluate complex performance tasks;
◆ Use your students' results to communicate more effectively with parents.

This must-have second edition is fully aligned to the Common Core State Standards and assessments and includes a variety of new performance tasks and rubrics, along with samples of student work. Additionally, downloadable student handout versions of all the performance tasks are available as free eResources from our website (www.routledge.com/97811389069891), so you can easily distribute them to your class.

Charlotte Danielson is an educational consultant now based in San Francisco, California. She has taught at all levels from kindergarten through college, and has worked as an administrator, a curriculum director, and a staff developer.

Pia Hansen was a classroom teacher for twenty-seven years, and is currently the Director of Professional Development for the Math Learning Center.

Math Performance Tasks

**Performance Tasks and Rubrics for Early Elementary Mathematics:
Meeting Rigorous Standards and Assessments**
Charlotte Danielson and Pia Hansen

**Performance Tasks and Rubrics for Upper Elementary Mathematics:
Meeting Rigorous Standards and Assessments**
Charlotte Danielson and Joshua Dragoon

**Performance Tasks and Rubrics for Middle School Mathematics:
Meeting Rigorous Standards and Assessments**
Charlotte Danielson and Elizabeth Marquez

**Performance Tasks and Rubrics for High School Mathematics:
Meeting Rigorous Standards and Assessments**
Charlotte Danielson and Elizabeth Marquez

Performance Tasks and Rubrics for Early Elementary Mathematics

Meeting Rigorous Standards and Assessments

Second Edition

Charlotte Danielson and Pia Hansen

Routledge
Taylor & Francis Group

NEW YORK AND LONDON

Second edition published 2016
by Routledge
711 Third Avenue, New York, NY 10017

and by Routledge
2 Park Square, Milton Park, Abingdon, Oxon, OX14 4RN

Routledge is an imprint of the Taylor & Francis Group, an informa business

© 2016 Taylor & Francis

The right of Charlotte Danielson and Pia Hansen to be identified as authors of this work has been asserted by them in accordance with sections 77 and 78 of the Copyright, Designs and Patents Act 1988.

First edition published by Routledge 1997

Library of Congress Cataloging in Publication Data
Names: Danielson, Charlotte. | Powell, Pia Hansen, 1955-
Title: Performance tasks and rubrics for early elementary mathematics :
    meeting rigorous standards and assessments / by Charlotte Danielson and
    Pia Hansen.
Description: Second edition. | New York : Routledge, 2016.
Identifiers: LCCN 2015037985 | ISBN 9781138906891 (pbk.) |
    ISBN 9781315695310 (e-book)
Subjects: LCSH: Mathematics—Study and teaching (Primary)—Evaluation.
Classification: LCC QA135.5 .D244 2016 | DDC 372.7—dc23
LC record available at http://lccn.loc.gov/2015037985

ISBN: 978-1-138-90689-1 (pbk)
ISBN: 978-1-315-69531-0 (ebk)

Typeset in Palatino
by Swales & Willis Ltd, Exeter, Devon, UK

Printed and bound in the United States of America by Sheridan

To Kaitlynn, Kale and Kennedi

Contents

eResources

The student handout versions of the tasks in this book are available on our website as free eResources so that you can download and print them for classroom use. You can access the eResources by visiting the book product page on our website, www.routledge.com/9781138906891. Click on the tab that says "eResources" and select the files. They will begin downloading to your computer.

Meet the Authors

Charlotte Danielson is an internationally recognized expert specializing recently in the area of teacher effectiveness, focusing on the design of teacher evaluation systems that both ensure teacher quality and promote professional learning.

Charlotte began her career as an economist but soon realized her passion for education. She became a teacher and later worked as a curriculum director, staff developer, and instructional coach, and then later as an advisor on educational policy. Her work in classroom-based assessment—in particular in the design and interpretation of performance tasks—served as a prototype for her later work in the analysis of teacher performance.

After years in the classroom, Charlotte realized that clear standards of practice were essential to advancing the profession. She wrote the *Framework for Teaching*, initially published in 1996 and intended to define good practice, primarily to inform professional learning and only later used as a tool for teacher evaluation. As such, it has, in many places, transformed school culture. She then began advising school districts, states, and countries on how to incorporate principles of professional learning into their evaluation systems.

Charlotte currently advises State Education Departments and National Ministries and Departments of Education, both in the United States and overseas. She is a sought-after keynote speaker at national and international conferences, and a policy consultant to legislative and administrative bodies. She continues to base her work on a profound awareness of the complexity of teaching, the nature of learning, and the need to work to advance the professionalism of teaching.

Pia Hansen has been a classroom teacher for twenty-seven years, teaching students from pre-school to college level. Currently, she is the Director of Professional Development for the Math Learning Center and collaborates with teachers and districts on best practices. She is also the author of *The Mathematics Coaching Handbook, Second Edition*, published by Routledge Eye On Education. Pia is a recipient of the Presidential Award for Excellence in Elementary Mathematics Teaching.

Foreword

In June of 2010, the National Governors Association (NGA) and the Council Chief State School Officers (CCSSO) released the Common Core State Standards for Mathematics. The release of this set of "next generation" standards has profoundly influenced the vision and practice of mathematics education throughout the nation. In specifying the content of mathematics to be taught across the grades, CCSS for Mathematics stress conceptual understanding along with procedural skill. These new standards have introduced eight Standards for Mathematical Practice to highlight the importance of thinking mathematically and applying mathematical reasoning to address real world issues and problems. Many states have adopted the Common Core mathematics standards directly, while others have revised their previous mathematics standards to be more closely aligned with the CCSS.

Through its call for a greater emphasis on problem solving, reasoning, and mathematical communication, these new core standards unambiguously support the expanded use of performance tasks for classroom instruction and assessment. Indeed, effective performance tasks call for the Mathematical Practices by engaging students in applying mathematical concepts and ways of thinking in the context of tackling "authentic" problems.

While the emphases of these new core standards are clear, a number of practical questions remain: How do teachers develop "authentic" tasks to assess students' understanding and mathematical reasoning? How does the use of performance tasks fit with more traditional forms of assessment in mathematics? How do teachers evaluate student responses since performance tasks typically call for more than a single, correct answer?

Charlotte Danielson and Pia Hansen offer timely and practical answers in this readable guide to the development and use of performance tasks and rubrics in early elementary classrooms. The book provides an excellent overview of the rationale for, and the strengths and limitations of, the use of performance tasks to assess student achievement and progress in mathematics. They offer a user-friendly, field-tested process for developing performance tasks and rubrics, along with practical advice for evaluating student work, selecting "anchors," and establishing performance standards. Finally, the sample tasks, rubrics and student work samples provide tried and true resources for immediate use, while serving as models to guide development of additional tasks and scoring tools.

Readers of *Performance Tasks and Rubrics for Early Elementary Mathematics* will not be confronted with an ivory tower treatise on what should be. Rather, they will discover a valuable resource, grounded in the wisdom of years of experience in schools and classrooms, for making the vision of the new core standards come to life.

Jay McTighe
Educational Author and Consultant

Preface

Educators have long recognized the unique role and importance of assessment in the classroom environment. Assessment provides valuable information for both teachers and students regarding how well everyone is doing. Students can see where they went wrong in their understanding, and teachers can determine whether a concept needs to be re-taught or whether it should be taught differently. This function, of monitoring progress on important learning goals, is the first and most important purpose of assessment.

Assessment also defines what students must know and be able to do to succeed in a particular teacher's class. Students frequently say that they don't know, until they have seen a teacher's first tests in the fall, just what she values. Is she a stickler for details? Or are the big ideas all that is important? What teachers assess and how they assess it convey what is important, both to them and in the subject. This can serve a clarifying purpose for teachers as well as students. By specifying what their students should study and determining how best to elicit evidence of how well they know it, teachers make decisions about what is truly important. Through the assessments teachers design and the feedback they provide to students, teachers reveal, both explicitly and implicitly, their understanding of and beliefs about curriculum and standards.

Since the release of the first edition of this book the educational landscape has changed enormously. The No Child Left Behind Act (NCLB) mandated annual testing and performance targets for subgroups of students. Race to the Top led to shifts in teacher evaluation, promoted the adoption of the Common Core State Standards, and led to the creation of the PARCC and Smarter Balanced Assessment Consortia (also known as SBAC). When tests "count," they motivate as well. That is, to the extent that tests or other assessments are used to calculate students' grades, students will try to do well. Teachers are also held accountable for student performance on standardized tests and other measures of achievement as a result of the changes to teacher evaluation in recent years. Some states and school districts use test scores as the basis for rewards or sanctions. In whatever ways test scores matter, teachers want their students to do well. Most teachers will provide instruction that supports their students' success on these tests, especially when stakes are high.

Tests and other assessments influence practice by defining important content. But the form of an assessment matters as well. That is, when students are asked on tests (and know in advance that they will be asked) to answer a number of multiple-choice or short-answer questions, they tend to prepare in that manner, committing to memory that which they predict will be on the test. If deeper understanding is not required for the test, they may not strive to achieve it. If a question is ambiguous, they will seek to "read the mind" of the teacher, to determine the right answer even if they believe another is better. The form of assessment also affects teachers' practices. If a test does not require, or does not reward, understanding, why should teachers emphasize it in their own classrooms, particularly since it typically requires more instructional time than rote teaching? If all that is needed in mathematics, for example, is for students to get the right answer (possibly without understanding why the procedure works) then the procedure is all that will be provided in some classrooms.

However, if assessment is designed to gauge deeper understanding, students will work to show what they know, even if they are unable to reach a single, correct answer. In contrast with multiple-choice questions that comprise the bulk of most large-scale, standardized tests, the heart of the assessment practices espoused in this text reflect the belief that learning isn't an all-or-nothing proposition. Assessment has the power to reveal where along a trajectory of learning a student currently is so that he or she may be supported in moving further along that trajectory. And assessments can reveal important things about students' understandings and their misconceptions. Assessments matter, therefore, both in what they assess and how they assess it. The content of a test affects what students study and teachers teach, and the form of the assessment affects how they approach the task. Teachers have discovered, for example, that if they want their students to become better writers, they must make good writing count in the classroom; they must teach it systematically and assess it authentically. A test of correcting errors, for example, will not do; they must assess students' actual writing. Similarly, if teachers want students to acquire skills in solving mathematical problems, or communicating their mathematical ideas, they must both teach and assess those skills.

These considerations have provided much of the energy behind the movement towards "performance assessment," that is, students actually creating or constructing an answer to a question. Teachers and policy-makers alike have discovered that when assessment tasks more accurately mirror the types of learning goals they have for students—both in the content and the form of assessment—the learning environment is transformed. The assessments themselves tend to be motivational and engaging: students invest energy in the tasks and commit to them. In addition, performance assessments even serve to educate as well as assess student learning. Students learn from doing performance tasks.

However, performance assessment has one enormous drawback: it is time-consuming to do, both to design and to work into classroom instructional time. Even teachers who are committed to the practice of performance assessment find that they don't have time to design good performance tasks, to try them out with students, and perfect them for later use. Furthermore, most teachers have only limited experience designing performance tasks and scoring rubrics as part of their professional preparation. And even when educators have learned such skills as part of their continuing professional growth, they may lack the confidence to use such performance tasks as a central part of their assessment plan.

This book is designed to address this need. It is based on the assumption that many educators are interested in incorporating performance assessment into their classroom routines, but have either not yet acquired the technical skill or do not have the time required to design them on their own. This book provides a collection of performance tasks and scoring rubrics for a number of topics in early elementary mathematics, which teachers can use as is, or adapt for their students and their particular situation. It is intended to save time for busy educators, to provide examples of tested performance tasks. The samples of student work provide a range of responses, to clarify the tasks, and to anchor the points on the scoring rubrics.

Chapter 1 provides the reader with an introduction to performance assessment and how it is distinguished from traditional testing. Chapter 2 offers a rationale for performance assessment, explaining its strengths (and its drawbacks) as compared with more traditional approaches. In Chapter 3 the reader can find guidance in making an evaluation plan, and linking that plan to the overall approach to curriculum development. Chapter 4 shares criteria for quality performance tasks. Chapter 5 offers a step-by-step procedure for creating and adapting a performance task for classroom use, and Chapter 6 provides an overview of how scoring rubrics can be used to evaluate complex performance. In Chapter 7, a process for the design and adaptation of rubrics is shared. Chapter 8 is the heart of the collection, and offers performance tasks (some with annotated student work) and rubrics, covering the major topics in early elementary mathematics, designed to be adapted, or used as is, in your classroom. The Routledge website, www.routledge.com/9781138906891, contains student handouts of each of the 20 tasks, so that you can print and copy them for classroom use.

Acknowledgments

The authors acknowledge with special appreciation the extensive amount of guidance, encouragement, and editorial insight provided by Lauren Davis, Senior Editor in Education at Routledge. She helped us make the revisions necessary to make the books in this series current, relevant, and useful to teachers.

We would also like to thank Jay McTighe for his thoughtful Foreword, as well as the reviewers who looked at the first edition and made suggestions for updates.

1

Introduction

What Is Performance Assessment?

This book concerns the classroom use of performance assessment, and the evaluation of student work in response to performance tasks. It contains a collection of performance tasks in early elementary school mathematics, but also includes guidance for educators to design or adapt performance tasks for their own use and to be a wise consumer of performance tasks that may be available to them.

While performance assessment is essential to a well-rounded assessment plan, it should not be used exclusively. Other item types associated with traditional testing have an important role to play, particularly in assessing a large domain or evaluating student knowledge. But in assessing student understanding, in order to ascertain how well students can apply their knowledge, some type of performance assessment is essential.

In this book, performance assessment means any assessment of student learning that requires the evaluation of student writing, products, or behavior. That is, it includes all assessment with the exception of multiple choice, matching, true/false testing, or problems with a single correct answer. Classroom-based performance assessment includes all such assessment that occurs in the classroom for formative or summative purposes and is evaluated by teachers as distinct from large-scale, state-wide testing programs.

Performance assessment is fundamentally criterion-referenced rather than norm-referenced. That is, teachers who adopt performance assessment are concerned with the degree to which students can demonstrate knowledge and skill in a certain field. They know what it means to demonstrate competence; the purpose of a performance assessment is to allow students to show what they can do. The criteria for evaluating performance are important; teachers use their professional judgment in establishing such criteria and defining levels of performance. And the standards they set for student performance are typically above those expected for minimal competency; they define accomplished performance.

Norm-referenced tests are less valuable to teachers than are performance assessments. True, teachers may learn what their students can do compared to other students of the same age. However, the items on the test may or may not reflect the curriculum of a given school or district; to the extent that these are different, the information provided may not be of value to the teacher. Moreover, the results of most standardized tests are not known for some time. Even for those items included in a school's curriculum, it does not help a teacher to know in June that a student did not know, in April, a concept that was taught the previous November. Of what possible use is that information to the teacher in June? It may not even still be true. And even if true, the information comes too late to be useful.

In addition, the only way students demonstrate progress on a norm-referenced test is in comparison to other students. Progress per se is not shown as progress. That is, a student's standing may move from the 48th percentile to the 53rd percentile. However, the student may not have learned much but other students may have learned less! So while norm-referenced tests have their value, for example for large-scale program evaluation, they are of limited use to teachers who want to know what each of their students have learned with respect to the Common Core State Standards or any set of standards that guides their curriculum. Performance assessment, then, is criterion-referenced. It reflects the curriculum goals of a teacher, school, or district with respect to the set of standards that guides their curriculum, and when used in the context of classroom teaching, it informs instructional decisions.

The remaining sections of this chapter describe the different uses and types of performance assessment.

The Uses of Classroom-Based Performance Assessment

Assessment of student learning in the classroom is done for many purposes and can serve many ends. When teachers design or choose their assessment strategies, it is helpful to determine, at the outset, which of the many possible uses they have in mind. Some possibilities are described here.

Instructional Decision-Making

Many teachers discover, after they have taught a concept, that many students didn't "get it"; that, while they may have had looks of understanding on their faces, and may have participated in the instructional activities, they are unable to demonstrate the knowledge or understanding on their own.

This is important information for teachers to have, as they determine what to do next with a class, or even with a few students. They may decide that they must re-teach the concept, or create a different type of instructional activity. Alternatively, if only a few students lack understanding, a teacher might decide to work with them separately, or to design an activity that can be used for peer tutoring.

Whatever course of action a teacher decides upon, however, it is decided on the basis of information regarding student understanding. That implies that the assessment strategies used will reveal student understanding, or lack of it. When used for instructional decision-making, it is the teacher alone who uses the information to determine whether the instructional activities achieved their intended purpose.

Feedback to Students

Performance assessment, like any assessment, may also be used to provide feedback to students regarding their progress. Depending on how it is constructed, a performance task can let students know in which dimensions of performance they excel, and in which they need to devote additional energy. Such feedback is, by its nature, individualized; the feedback provided to one student will be very different from that provided to another if their performances are different. It is efficient for the teacher, however, since the important dimensions of performance have been identified beforehand.

Communication with Families

Actual student performance on well-designed tasks can provide families with authentic evidence of their child's level of functioning. Many families are skeptical of tests that they don't understand, and are not sure of the meaning of numbers, percentiles and scaled scores. But student answers to an open-ended question or to other performance assessments are easy to understand and can serve to demonstrate to families the level of understanding of their child. These samples of student work are highly beneficial for open house or conferences, serving to educate family members and to validate the judgments of the teacher.

Such indication of student performance is of particular importance if a teacher is concerned about a child and wants to persuade a parent/guardian that action is needed. It is impossible for parents, when confronted with the work of their own child, to question the commitment of the teacher in meeting that child's needs. Whether the work is exemplary and the teacher is recommending a more advanced placement, or the work reveals little understanding, the actual samples of student performance are invaluable to a teacher in making a case for action.

Summative Evaluation of Student Learning

In addition to having formative purposes, a performance assessment may be used to evaluate student learning and may contribute to decisions regarding grades. The issue of grading is complex and will be addressed more fully on page 17 of this book, but the results from performance tasks, like any assessment, can serve to substantiate a teacher's judgment in assigning a grade.

Different Types of Classroom-Based Assessment

Assessment takes many forms, depending on the types of instructional goals being assessed, and the use to which the assessment will be put. The major types are presented in Table 1.1, and are described in the following sections.

Summative Assessments

Summative assessments have always been (and will continue to be) an important method for ascertaining what students *know* and can do.

When teachers decide to move to more authentic aspects of performance in order to evaluate student learning, they do not necessarily abandon traditional types of summative assessments. On the contrary, they may use traditional tests or item types for that which they are well suited (for example, for sampling knowledge), recognizing their substantial strengths as a methodology. However, when teachers want to measure the depth, rigor, and complexity of comprehension they may use summative assessments which include performance tasks or technology-enhanced items or extended constructed-response items. Of course, summative as well as formative assessments may include both traditional and non-traditional item types.

Summative assessments are generally given to students under what we call "testing conditions," that is, conditions that ensure that we are actually getting the authentic work of individuals and that the experience is the same for all students. Testing conditions are:

◆ *Limited time.* Generally speaking, time for a test is strictly limited. Students must complete the test within a certain amount of time (frequently a class period, but sometimes more or less than that). This provision ensures that some students don't devote far greater time to the assignments than others.

◆ *Limited (or no) resources.* Although there are exceptions to this rule (such as open-book tests and the use of calculators), students taking a test are usually not permitted to consult materials as they work. An insistence on no additional resources rules out, of course, trips to the library while taking a test. This provision ensures that what students produce on the test reflects only their own understanding.

◆ *No talking with peers or looking at others' papers.* When taking a test, it is important that students produce their own work. Unless teachers adhere to this condition, they are never sure whether what they receive from an individual student reflects that student's understanding, or that of his or her friends.

Table 1.1 Forms of Classroom-Based Assessment

Assessment Types	
Formative: Both formal and informal ongoing assessment of *student learning* that provides evidence used by teachers to adjust instruction and by students to improve their learning. When informal, it allows for observation of spontaneous behavior.	*Summative*: Formal assessment given periodically to determine what students know and can do with respect to some standard or benchmark, e.g., end-of-unit test, midterm exam, final project.
Item Types **(may appear on a formative or a summative assessment)**	
Traditional items (may appear on a formative or a summative assessment)	*Non-traditional items** (may appear on a formative or a summative assessment) Results in a physical or written product and allows for observation of structured or spontaneous behavior
◆ Selected response: multiple choice, matching, and true/false questions ◆ Fill in the blanks ◆ Solve without showing the process ◆ Short constructed response	◆ Performance tasks ◆ Extended constructed response ◆ Technology-enhanced

Note: *For the purposes of this book, extended constructed response and all non-traditional assessment is considered performance assessment.

In addition, summative assessments are traditionally of two basic types: selected response and constructed response.

- ◆ *Selected response.* In a selected-response test, students select the best answer from those given. True/false and matching tests may also be included in this category. Short-answer items are technically constructed-response items (since the student supplies the answer), but since there is generally a single right answer, such items are a special case, and share more characteristics in their scoring with multiple-choice items.
- ◆ *Constructed response.* In a constructed-response test, students answer a question in their own words. Open-ended questions are constructed response, as are essay questions on a test.

Of course, a single summative assessment may contain a combination of selected-response and constructed-response items. In fact, most tests do: they generally consist of some multiple-choice, true/false, short-answer, or matching items for a portion of the test and several constructed-response items for the remainder. The balance between these different types of test items varies enormously, by subject, grade level, and the preference of the teacher.

Formative Assessments

Unlike summative assessments, formative assessments are an ongoing part of the instructional process in which evidence is collected either formally or informally of student engagement with mathematical concepts, skills, and processes. As incorporated into classroom practice, formative assessment provides teachers with evidence of student understanding that they can use to determine next steps in instruction in a timely fashion. For example, if teachers observe student behavior that reveals a misconception, they can make an on-the-spot intervention, or if a teacher gathers evidence through a formal classroom assessment, the results of that assessment can be determined within a day or two with appropriate interventions taken.

Performance assessment is most often associated with formative assessment but performance assessment such as extended constructed-response items are increasingly becoming part of classroom-based and standardized summative assessments.

Product

A product is any item produced by students which is evaluated according to established criteria and can be the result of either a formative or summative

> ☑ **Professional Development Tip**
>
> **Focus on Formative Assessment**
>
> Identification and discussion of types of formative assessments, both formal and informal, can be helpful to teachers. For instance, just knowing that formative assessment can be as simple as a check for understanding or as complex as analysis of a test in order to determine the level at which a student is progressing in their understanding of mathematics. Having teachers demonstrate the specific ways that they check for understanding, or analyze test results, or use assessment results to determine next steps in instruction can be of great help to other teachers. For instance, it can help a teacher understand the most effective way to check for understanding— e.g., nodding heads to indicate understanding versus using exit tickets to find out what students know. Examining the differences between summative and formative assessment is also a useful exercise. For instance, it is important to understand that if the results of an assessment, no matter how small, are not used to inform instruction, it cannot be formative.

performance assessment. A product is a thing, a physical object, and is often (but not always) produced by students outside of school time. Students may take as long as they want and need to, and may consult books and speak with other people. Products may be one of two types: written or physical.

- *Written products.* A written product may be a term paper, an essay for homework, a journal entry, a drama, or a lab report. It is anything written by students, but not under testing conditions.
- *Physical products.* A physical product may be, for example, a diorama, a science construction, a project in industrial arts, or a sculpture. Physical products are three-dimensional things, and take up space.

Some projects done by students represent a combination of written and physical products. For example, most science fair projects consist of a physical construction of some sort, combined with a written description of the scientific principles involved.

Products are a rich source of information for teachers in seeking to understand what their students know and can do. However, they have two significant disadvantages, which limit their usefulness for high-stakes assessment. The first relates to authenticity. When a student turns in a project, the teacher has no way of knowing the degree to which the work reflects the student's own knowledge and understanding, and the degree to which the student's families or older siblings might have assisted. The second disadvantage is that while a product may enable students to demonstrate depth of understanding, they don't accomplish what most assessments must do, namely to sample the breadth of knowledge and skill.

For instructional purposes, most teachers encourage their students to obtain as much help as they can get; students are bound to learn more from an assignment with the insights of additional people. However, for purposes of assessment we need to know what each student can do; this requirement limits the usefulness of out-of-class assignments for evaluation. When used, they should be supplemented by other sources of information (for example, an assignment given under testing conditions) of which the teacher can be sure of authorship.

Behavior

Lastly, students demonstrate their knowledge or skill through their behavior, and this behavior can be evaluated. Behavior is that aspect of student performance which does not result in a tangible object; once completed, it is finished. However, behavior may be captured and stored, and then evaluated, and as such can be the result of either a formative or summative performance assessment. For example, a skit may be video recorded, or a student reading aloud may be audio recorded. There are two types of behavior that may be used for evaluation:

- *Structured behavior.* In structured behavior, students are performing according to a pre-established framework. They may be staging a debate or a panel discussion. They may be giving a skit, performing a dance, or making a presentation. Teachers may be interviewing their students. Drama and speech classes depend on this type of performance to evaluate learning; it is useful in other fields as well. In virtually every state, acquiring a driver's license depends on successful performance behind the wheel, and assessments in world languages typically include a spoken portion.
- *Spontaneous behavior.* Students can also reveal their understanding through their spontaneous behavior. For example, their interaction when working on group projects, their questions during a discussion and their choices during free time, all demonstrate important aspects of their learning.

Because of the unstructured nature of spontaneous behavior, it is useful primarily as a supplemental form of assessment. However, for certain types of instructional goals, such as skill in collaboration, it may be the only appropriate form. The documentation of spontaneous behavior depends on careful observation. Many teachers use checklists so they can make their "kid watching" as systematic as possible. Spontaneous behavior is most often associated with formative assessment.

Chapter Summary

◆ Classroom-based performance assessment is criterion-referenced and is used to evaluate student learning on clearly identified instructional goals with respect to the Common Core State Standards or any set of standards that guides their curriculum. As such, it should be designed to be of optimal usefulness to its different audiences: teachers, students, and parents.

◆ Classroom-based assessment may be used for several different purposes. An overall assessment plan will take all desired purposes into account.

◆ There are different types of classroom assessment. The major types are formative assessments and summative assessments, either of which can include performance assessments resulting in various products and behavior. Depending on the types of instructional goals to be assessed, they are all valuable. For the purposes of this book all assessment except selected-response assessments are considered performance assessment.

2

Why Use Performance Assessment?

It is clear that the design and implementation of performance assessment are far more time-consuming than the use of traditional tests. Why, one might ask, should a busy educator go to the trouble of changing? A good question, and one that deserves a thoughtful answer.

First, it should be made clear that when teachers use performance assessment, they don't stop using traditional forms of assessment. Traditional forms of assessments will always be with us, and they should be. It is frequently important to ascertain what students know about a subject; alternatively, we must be sure that they have read an assignment. There is no substitute for a traditional type of quiz or test to ascertain these things. But as a steady diet, traditional assessments have serious limitations. These are described below.

The Limitations of Traditional Testing

When we refer to "traditional testing" in this book, we mean multiple-choice, true/false, matching, or short-answer assessments that teachers create or adapt for use in their classrooms. These are generally provided by the publishers of text programs, or have evolved over time. As noted above, they are useful for certain purposes (and they are certainly efficient to score), but when used exclusively, they have a negative influence.

Validity

The most serious criticism of traditional testing is that the range of student knowledge and skill that can be tested is extremely limited. Many aspects of understanding to which teachers and their communities are most committed simply don't lend themselves to multiple-choice assessment. To illustrate this point, it is helpful to identify the different categories of educational purposes (instructional goals) and to consider how they can be assessed.

There are, of course, many different ways to classify goals for this type of analysis; one comprehensive classification scheme is outlined below.

◆ *Knowledge.* Most types of knowledge, whether procedural knowledge (i.e., how to wash lab equipment), conceptual understanding (i.e., the meaning of slope), and the application of knowledge (i.e., determining the amount of paint needed to paint a room), may all be assessed through traditional means. Indeed, it is in the assessment of knowledge that traditional assessment rightfully exerts its strongest influence.

 Conceptual understanding, however, is not ideally suited to traditional testing since students can memorize, for example, a definition of "slope" without really understanding it; their lack of understanding might not be revealed through a multiple-choice or matching test. It is only through their explanation of the concept in their own words, or their use of the concept in a problem that their understanding, or lack of it, is demonstrated.

◆ *Reasoning.* Traditional testing is poorly suited to the assessment of reasoning. While it is true that well-designed multiple-choice tests may be used to evaluate pure logic, most teachers without technical skills in this area are not advised to attempt it. Most of the reasoning we care about in schools (i.e., analyzing data, formulating and testing hypotheses, recognizing patterns) is better assessed through nontraditional means.

◆ *Communication.* In order to know whether students can communicate, we must ask them to do so in writing or speaking. Attempts are made, of course, to evaluate students' understanding of written text and spoken language through multiple-choice tests. To some extent these attempts are successful but they rarely give teachers information they did not already have through more informal means. For the productive aspects of communication writing and speaking—there is no substitute for students actually writing and speaking, and then evaluating their performance.

◆ *Skills*. Social skills and psychomotor skills are completely unsuited to traditional forms of assessment. A multiple-choice test on the rules of basketball does not tell a teacher whether or not a student can dribble the ball. And a matching test on how to work in groups does not convey whether students have actually acquired skills in collaboration. Nothing short of observation will do, using a carefully prepared observation guide. To the extent that skills are important aspects of learning, teachers must employ nontraditional assessment methods.

◆ *Affective Areas*. As with skills, traditional testing is entirely unsuited to the assessment of the affective domain. To the extent that teachers attempt to cultivate students' productive dispositions towards work (for example, habits of mind, reasoning and communication, attending to precision, and perseverance) they must look for little indicators through student behavior. As teachers try to cultivate mathematical practices in their students, like making sense of problems and persevering in solving them, they must look for little comments and signs from their students. Other aspects of the affective domain are equally ill-matched to traditional testing, from self-confidence, to traits such as honesty and respect for private property, through the ability to weigh ethical arguments. In short, life and career skills such as those as defined by the Partnership for 21st Century Skills are best assessed by non-traditional assessment.

As is evident from the descriptions above, if teachers use only traditional forms of assessment, they will be unable to assess many aspects (some would say the most important aspects) of student learning. Clearly, other methods such as constructed-response tests, projects, and behavior are needed. These alternative modes must therefore be designed and procedures developed for the evaluation of student work produced through these alternative means.

Design Issues

Measurement experts argue that most aspects of student knowledge and skill may be assessed through well-designed multiple-choice tests. They point to well-known tests that evaluate problem solving, reasoning, and data analysis. On further examination, by looking at the actual items, most teachers would probably agree that the items require some higher-level thinking on the part of students.

Teachers should not assume because such test items are possible to construct that they themselves can construct them, or should want to spend the necessary time to do so. These test items are designed by measurement experts and are extensively field-tested to ensure that they are both valid and reliable. Neither of these conditions is available to most practicing educators, who have their next day's lessons to think about.

When teachers try to design their own multiple-choice tests, they encounter three related, though somewhat distinct, difficulties:

◆ *Ambiguity*. A major challenge confronting test developers is to create multiple-choice test items in which the wrong answers are plausible and yet unambiguously wrong. Ideally, the distractors (the wrong answers) should be incorrect in ways in which students' thinking is typically flawed, so a student's pattern of wrong answers may reveal diagnostic information.

Such tests are very difficult to construct. Most teachers have had the experience of creating a test in which students can, by guessing or using a process of elimination, determine the right answer even when they know very little about the subject.

◆ *Authenticity*. In order to engage students in meaningful work, it is helpful for assessment to be as authentic as possible. Students are more likely to produce work of good quality if the questions seem plausible and worthwhile. But to design an authentic multiple-choice test, one that elicits the desired knowledge and skill, is very difficult. Highly authentic questions tend to be long and cumbersome, while more focused questions are often found to be boring and inauthentic by students.

◆ *Time*. Good multiple-choice questions require a great deal of time to create. And unless they are tested before being used, teachers cannot be sure that they are valid. That is, the question may be ambiguous, or several of the choices may be plausible. Hence, students are justified in challenging such questions and the evaluations based on them.

These factors, taken together, suggest that teachers are unlikely to be successful in creating their own multiple-choice tests for complex learning. Experts in test design can succeed more often than novices, but even experts are limited in what is possible through the technique.

Influence on Instruction

Probably the most serious concern about the exclusive use of traditional testing relates to its effect on the instructional process. Since traditional tests are best suited to the assessment of low-level knowledge, such instructional goals are heavily represented (to the virtual exclusion of other, more complex, learning goals) in such tests. This is why some standardized tests are using performance assessment along with traditional assessment to determine what students know and can do with respect to a particular set of standards.

It is well known that "what you test is what you get." Through our assessment methods we convey to students what is important to learn. And when the tests we give reflect only factual or procedural knowledge, we signal to students that such knowledge is more important than their ability to reason, to solve problems, to work together collaboratively, or to write effectively. Since multiple-choice tests are best at evaluating students' command of factual knowledge, many students think that school learning is trivial, and never realize that their teachers value the expression of their own ideas, a creative approach to problems, or the design of an imaginative experiment.

The most powerful means teachers have at their disposal for shifting the culture of their classrooms to one of significant work is to change their assessment methodologies. While traditional tests will always have a value, combining their use with alternative means sends an important signal to students regarding what sort of learning is valued in school. If good ideas and imaginative projects count, students will begin to shift their conceptions of the meaning of school.

The Benefits of Performance Assessment

Many of the advantages of performance assessment are simply the reverse side of the limitations of traditional testing, namely, that they enable teachers to assess students in all those aspects of learning they value, in particular, writing and speaking, reasoning and problem solving, psychomotor and social skills, and the entire affective domain. However, there are many other benefits to be derived as well. These are described in the following sections.

Clarity as to Criteria and Standards
When teachers use performance assessment, they discover that they must be extremely clear, both to themselves and to their students, as to the criteria they will use to evaluate student work, and the standard of performance they expect. For many teachers, this clarity is greater than that required for traditional testing, and requires that they give sustained thought to difficult questions such as, "What do I really want my students to be able to do?" and, "What is most important in this unit?" and, "How good is good enough?"

These questions, while some of the most important that teachers ever consider, tend to be obscured by the pressure of daily work, and the normal routines of life in schools. The design of performance assessment tasks puts them at the center. Most teachers find that, while the questions are difficult to answer, their entire instructional program is greatly strengthened as a result of the effort.

Professional Dialogue about Criteria and Standards

If teachers create their performance assessments together, they must decide together how they will evaluate student work and what their standards will be. These are not easy discussions, but most teachers find them to be extremely valuable.

Occasionally, teachers find that their criteria for problem solving, for example, are very different from one another. One teacher may believe that the process used is more important than whether or not the answer is correct. Another may believe the reverse. They must resolve their differences in designing a problem solving task if they are to evaluate student work together. On the other hand, they could agree to disagree, and each use his or her own procedure. But the conversation will have been valuable in isolating such a fundamental difference in approach.

Improved Student Work

Virtually all teachers report improved quality of student work when they begin using performance assessment. This is due, no doubt, to several factors:

- *Clarity as to criteria and standards.* Just as greater clarity in criteria and standards is valuable to teachers and contributes to professional dialogue, it is essential for students. When students know what is expected, they are far more likely to be able to produce it than if they do not.
- *Greater confidence in work.* When students understand the criteria and standards to be used in evaluating their work, they can approach it with greater confidence. The criteria provide them with guidelines for their work and they can estimate the time required to produce work of good quality. All this tends to increase student engagement and pride in their work.
- *High expectations.* When they make the standards for exemplary performance clear to students, teachers are sending an important signal about their expectations. They are saying to students, in effect, "Here is how I define excellence. Anyone here can produce work of such quality by applying sufficient effort." This is a powerful message for students; it brings excellence within their reach.

◆ *Greater student engagement.* When students are involved in performance tasks, particularly those that are highly authentic, they are more likely to be highly motivated in their work than if they are answering trivial types of questions. As a consequence of this engagement, the quality of student work is generally high.

Improved Communication with Families

Student work produced as part of a performance assessment is extremely meaningful to parents. If collected in a portfolio and used for conferences, these products can serve to document student learning (or its lack). If necessary, a student's work may be shown to families next to that of another (anonymous) student, to illustrate differences in performance. Such documentation may be very helpful to teachers in persuading a parent/guardian of the need for additional educational services.

If student work as part of performance assessment is maintained in a portfolio, however, the selections should be made with care. There are many possible uses of a portfolio, and students can benefit from the reflection that accompanies their own selection of "best work" entries. But as a documentation of student progress, items should be chosen that reflect student performance in all the important instructional goals. For example, if a math program consists of 5 strands taught through 12 units, the selections made should document each of the units, and all of the strands. These issues will be discussed more fully in Chapter 3.

☑ **Professional Development Tip**

Analyzing Types of Assessments

A discussion of the advantages and disadvantages of both traditional and non-traditional assessments can help teachers create or choose the kind of assessments that will elicit the evidence they need to make sound instructional decisions. Having teachers create a few selected-response items and a few performance assessment items targeting a skills-based standard, such as solving a linear equation, and a cognitively based standard, such as distinguishing between situations that can be modeled with linear functions and with exponential functions, will enhance their understanding of assessment. Individually scoring prepared responses to those items as they see fit and then comparing scores is likely to be quite interesting as the scores will probably be quite different. This can then lead the way to understanding the need for a commonly agreed upon rubric when scoring performance assessments, which will be discussed further in Chapter 6.

A Word about Grading

Many educators ask about converting the results of performance assessment to traditional grades. There are no easy answers to this question for the simple reason that the issue of grading does not lend itself to simplistic approaches. The reasons for this difficulty, however, are not related to performance assessment, but to the varied methods and purposes for assigning grades.

A "score" on a performance assessment is a straightforward matter; student work is evaluated against a clear standard and a judgment made as to where it stands against that standard. If students' grades are also intended (solely) to reflect the degree of mastery of the curriculum, then the score on the performance assessment can be translated in a fairly linear way to a grade. A score of "4" could be an "A," a "3" could be a "B," and so forth.

However, there are several reasons why such a procedure may not be ideal. For one thing, most teachers use other methods in addition to performance tasks to assess student learning. The typical evaluation plan used by a teacher will include traditional tests as well as performance items. Therefore, the results from different methods must be combined in some manner, including weighting some items more than others.

In addition, many teachers incorporate other elements in addition to achievement against a standard into a grade. They may want to build in the degree of progress from earlier work, for example, or the amount of effort or discipline displayed by a student. Alternatively, teachers may have offered some students a lot of coaching in their performance assessments (thereby using them also as teaching tools) and they may recognize that the students' performance reflects more than what they could do on their own.

Therefore, while performance assessments may not translate directly into grades, it may be a good idea to establish some connection between them, making the necessary provision for combining scores on different assessments. If this is done, it sends powerful messages to students. Primarily, such a procedure takes the mystery out of grading, and allows students to know in advance the criteria by which their work will be evaluated. In addition, it also conveys to students that high grades are within the reach of all students. Over time they recognize that if they work hard, they (all of them) can do well. This fosters a growth mindset (see Carol Dweck (2007) *Mindset: The New Psychology of Success*). In this situation, good grades are not rationed; all students whose work is at the highest standard can get an "A." As students come to internalize this awareness, and act upon it, it can transform a classroom into a far more purposeful place, and one in which students are concerned with the quality of their work.

Chapter Summary

◆ Traditional forms of assessment carry many disadvantages, which, when such tests are used exclusively, undermine the best intentions of teachers. These tests can evaluate only a narrow band of student learning and, even within that band, are extremely difficult to construct well.

◆ The use of performance assessment contributes many important benefits, beyond strictly measurement issues, to the culture of a classroom. These advantages are derived from clarity of criteria and standards, and benefit teachers, students, and parents.

3

Making an Evaluation Plan

Designing and implementing performance assessment entails a major investment of time and energy. To ensure that this investment is a wise one and that it yields the desired benefits, it is essential to work from a plan. How to develop such a plan and integrate it into a school or district's curriculum is the subject of this chapter.

A Curriculum Map

A useful approach to developing an assessment plan for mathematics instruction is to begin with a consideration of goals in the mathematics curriculum as a whole. An assessment plan, after all, should have as its goal the assessment of student learning in the curriculum; it makes no sense in isolation from the curriculum. Therefore, a plan for assessment should be created with the end in mind.

Critical Areas of Focus, Domains, and Clusters

A good place to start in thinking about the assessment demands of the Common Core and other rigorous state standards is to consider the domains/strands and major clusters. Critical areas are identified by grade level, to provide a focus, to prioritize what's worth teaching and re-teaching for mastery, and what is supporting the work of the next grade.

These standards have had an enormous influence on the teaching of mathematics, and have caused educators everywhere to think more deeply about what they teach and how to engage their students in both conceptual understanding and procedural fluency with duel intensity.

For example, kindergarten teachers are developing counting and cardinality concepts that are then applied in first and second grades in the Number and Operations in Base Ten domain, when students count multiples of 10, 100, and 5s from any given number to add and subtract. Fraction concepts, parts of a whole, are introduced in the Geometry domain in first grade (halves and fourths) and second grade (halves, thirds, and fourths). Students apply their understanding of equal parts to unit fractions on a number line in grade three and operations with fractions in grades four and five. These content standards define grade-level proficiency and mastery, with a focus on fewer concepts, with a deeper conceptual understanding. Teaching less, at a higher cognitive demand.

The eight Standards for Mathematical Practice describe the characteristics and traits of mathematically proficient students. These practices rest on important processes and proficiencies much like the National Council of Teachers of Mathematics (NCTM) process standards of problem solving, reasoning and proof, communication, representation and connections. They also reflect the proficiency specified in the National Research Council's report *Adding It Up*: adaptive reasoning, strategic competence, conceptual understanding (comprehension of mathematical concepts, operations and relations), procedural fluency (skill in carrying out procedures flexibly, accurately, efficiently, and appropriately), and productive disposition (habitual inclination to see mathematics as sensible, useful, and worthwhile, coupled with a belief in diligence and one's own efficacy).

Publishers, administrators, and teachers that recognize how fundamental the practices are to learning the new content standards, will certainly be interested in creating performance task assessments. Weaving the content standards with the practices has the potential to transform mathematical teaching and learning from what many experienced as students. Math content knowledge, the "what," must be addressed alongside of the "how" to support the belief that all students can—and must—develop proficiency with the mathematical practices.

School mathematics has traditionally been taught as a fixed set of facts and procedures for computing numerical and symbolic expressions to find one correct answer. Current practices are based on the beliefs that students should understand and reason with mathematical concepts, solve problems in diverse contexts, and develop a confidence in their own mathematical ability.

Active environments, where academic concepts are taught in a context of real-life problems, are more beneficial to students.

When educators are planning an intellectually stimulating curriculum for primary students that is rich in content, they look to the National Association for the Education of Young Children (NAEYC). Their recommendations for a high quality mathematics education are similar to the new practice standards:

◆ enhance children's natural interest in mathematics and their disposition to use it to make sense of their physical and social worlds;

◆ build on children's varying experiences, including their family, linguistic, and cultural backgrounds; their individual approaches to learning; and their informal knowledge;

◆ base mathematics curriculum and teaching practices on current knowledge of young children's cognitive, linguistic, physical, and social-emotional development;

◆ use curriculum and teaching practices that strengthen children's problem solving and reasoning processes as well as representing, communicating, and connecting mathematical ideas;

◆ ensure that the curriculum is coherent and compatible with known relationships and sequences of important mathematical ideas;

◆ provide for children's deep and sustained interaction with key mathematical ideas;

◆ integrate mathematics with other activities and other activities with mathematics;

◆ provide ample time, materials, and teacher support for children to engage in play, a context in which they explore and manipulate mathematical ideas with keen interest;

◆ actively introduce mathematical concepts, methods, and language through a range of appropriate experiences and teaching strategies;

◆ support children's learning by thoughtfully and continually assessing all children's mathematical knowledge, skills, and strategies.

(Source: http://www.naeyc.org/files/naeyc/file/
positions/Mathematics_Exec.pdf)

Primary teachers are aware of the stages of concept development with young children—exploration, inquiry, and utilization. Students actively explore all the possibilities in play. Then they are ready to participate in the introduction of numerical skill. The new learning takes on a totally new significance when students apply it to their own personal life. Students relate language to mathematical action and practice, communicating in a precise dialogue.

Concepts are constructed over time and children encounter an idea several times before they can begin to form generalizations. In Kindergarten, the concept of subtilizing, instantly recognizing sets without having to count each one, is developed over time with dice and domino patterns and scattered configurations. First graders begin to trust these sets/groups to count on, make combinations to 10 and learn double facts, without seeing each object and counting from 1. This understanding promotes computational fluency with mental strategies in second grade. Given multiple experiences, over time, with a variety of visual models, children generalize number concepts to solve word problems and bare number prompts efficiently, accurately and flexibly.

Although the new standards assign certain concepts to each grade level, due to the vast difference in children's previous experiences and development, some caution is required. It's not *when*, but *how* concepts are presented that allows all children access to understanding the big ideas in the mathematical curriculum. Manipulatives and visual models, language and play, are essential to student achievement.

The Developmental Stages of Mathematics

The *emerging mathematician* can recognize and identify numerals, use concrete and pictorial models to represent quantities, and use manipulatives to count. This child is able to sort and collect data with concrete materials, identify things that are longer and shorter, heavier and lighter, and recognize geometric shapes and determine if they are flat or solid.

The *beginning mathematician* can order and compare numbers, use concrete and abstract models to represent quantities, and begin to understand the relationship between addition and subtraction. This child is able to recall some basic facts to 10, represent and record data, measure things with nonstandard units, and compose and decompose geometric figures.

The *developing mathematician* can relate counting groups of objects to place value concepts, use abstract models to represent quantities, and use a variety of approaches to compute. This child is able to recall basic facts to 20, use place value thinking to compute with and without materials, generate, organize and analyze data, use standard measuring tools, and classify and sort two- and three-dimensional geometric shapes.

The *independent mathematician* can apply a well-developed understanding of mathematics to novel situations, recall number combinations, solve problems using algorithms, and compute two- and three-digit problems with more than one operation. This child is able to reflect on and improve the thinking processes necessary to compute, analyze data, measure, use precise math language to describe geometric shapes, and apply patterns and structure to new experiences.

These broad goals, outcomes, or strands provide the framework for curriculum planning. They do not comprise a curriculum; that is developed from the outcomes for each grade level. But they do offer guidance for those preparing the curricula at each stage.

Topics or Units

Most mathematics textbooks are still organized in a series of chapters or units, rather than clusters and standards. For example, in a typical second-grade mathematics text, the chapters might be:

- Addition Combinations to 20, Then 100, and Later 1,000
- Subtraction Combinations from 20, Then 100, and Later 1,000
- Place Value to 100 and Then 1,000
- Graphing (Picture Graphs, Bar Graphs, Line Plots)
- Telling Time
- Geometry
- Measurement
- Counting Money
- Fractions.

Clearly, some of the topics fit well with some of the standards. For example, the concepts taught in the "Units of Measure and Geometry" chapter address the goals in the "geometry" domain. But some of the other connections are not nearly so obvious. In which chapter, for instance, is material related to "mathematics as communication" or "modeling" found? If educators are committed to addressing all the goals stated or implied in the CCSSM Standards, or the equivalent document from their own state or district, then they must match the topics or units they teach with the goals inherent in those standards.

The best technique to use for this purpose is a matrix, such as is described in the next section, and a sample of which is presented in Table 3.1. This table focuses on the content standards for unit planning; however, teachers and curriculum planners should also keep the eight Standards for Mathematical Practice in mind as they create lessons.

Creating the Curriculum Map

Across the top of the matrix are listed the domains of the grade level. Down the left-hand side are listed all the topics or units in the year's curriculum, organized, insofar as can be known, in sequence. Then, for each unit or topic, teachers should consider which of the standards the topic addresses, and place a check mark in the corresponding box.

What results from this process is a map of the curriculum, demonstrating the ways in which the different domains, clusters, and standards are

Table 3.1 Curriculum/Assessment Planning Matrix

	Operations and Algebraic Thinking				Number & Operations in Base Ten		Measurement & Data			Geometry
Name of Unit	Represent and solve problems involving addition and subtraction	Understand and apply properties of operations and the relationship between addition and subtraction	Add and subtract within 20	Worth with addition and subtraction equations	Extend the counting sequence	Understand place value to add and subtract	Measure lengths indirectly and by iterating length units	Tell and write time	Represent and interpret data	Reason with shapes and their attributes
Example: *Adding and subtracting to 10*			✓ *(+ and – to 10 only)*							

(or can be, given the textbook in use) addressed in each of the topics of the curriculum. The map may reveal large gaps in the curriculum. If, for example, the curriculum map shows that some of the standards are not adequately addressed by the program in use, then some adjustments must be made to include supplements. It is also possible that the curriculum has content that is no longer relevant to that grade level. For example, probability. In which case, that content can be omitted in favor of the major work of the grade.

In some cases, the content might be aligned, but the Mathematical Practices are not developed in the lessons. For example, "reasoning and explaining" may be done exclusively by the teacher, and not an expectation for student behavior. In that case, educators have to determine in which topics they could develop that skill, and how. Once determined, they can then add check marks to the appropriate boxes. For instance, teachers could decide to add, to each of their units, a goal for modeling mathematics and using tools precisely, and identify the specific manipulatives and visual models they will use in the context of the lessons. In that way, they would adequately address all the content and practice standards.

Assessment Methodologies

Once the curriculum map has been produced, educators (teachers or curriculum specialists) must determine how each of the content and practice standards, and each of the clusters, are to be assessed. Some will lend themselves to traditional testing; others will require more complex performance assessment.

The Role of Traditional Testing

Some mathematics curriculum goals may be assessed through traditional testing. It is, and will always be, important for students to be able to perform accurate computations, to use technology to show they can identify attributes of geometric shapes and apply formulas. For all these reasons, educators would be ill-advised to abandon the use of traditional tests as part of their total assessment plan.

However, traditional testing is limited in what it can achieve. As teachers survey the curriculum map they have produced, they discover that some of the check marks they have written simply do not lend themselves to a multiple-choice or short-answer test. What kind of test, for example, could one construct that would assess students on the communication of ideas? Or on the use of models and tools?

Moreover, many educators argue that the use of traditional tests, even in those areas of the curriculum where they seem to be best suited, can do actual harm because some students, and their teachers, confuse procedural knowledge with conceptual understanding. That is, students learn a procedure, an algorithm, for getting "the right answer" with little or no understanding of how or why the procedure works, of where it would be useful, or of what the algorithm accomplishes. Therefore, they can take a test and solve problems correctly, but with poor conceptual understanding. And if the assessment procedures used do not reveal that lack of understanding, the students may move along to more complex concepts, ones that build on the previous ones, with an increasingly shaky foundation.

Thus, while traditional tests may be highly useful in assessing certain aspects of the mathematics curriculum, they should be used with caution and with full awareness of their limitations.

The Place for Performance Assessment

Performance assessment is the technique of choice for evaluating student understanding of much of the mathematics curriculum. When students are asked to complete a task—when they are asked to explain their thinking—they reveal their understanding of complex topics.

Sometimes performance assessment in mathematics can consist of a small addition to traditional testing. For example, students might be asked to solve a fairly traditional problem, but then asked to explain why they selected the approach they did. Their explanation reveals their understanding of the process, or their lack of it, and serves to assess their skill in the communication of mathematical ideas.

In addition, the authentic application of mathematical procedures is highly motivational to students. Many students regard the mundane problems (word problems) that they encounter in most mathematics textbooks with disbelief; their reaction is frequently one of "who cares?" With some thought, however, most teachers can create situations that students in their classes might actually encounter, which require the application of the mathematical ideas included in a given unit. The creation or adaption of such a task is the subject of Chapter 5.

A Plan to Get Started

The idea of creating (or even adapting) performance tasks for all those areas of the mathematics curriculum for which they would be well suited can be daunting. After all, if students as well as teachers are unfamiliar with such an approach, it is likely to take more time than planned. And because it is unfamiliar, everyone involved is likely to encounter unexpected difficulties. How, then, should one begin?

Not all standards are created equal, as indicated in Dr. Norman Webb's Depth of Knowledge (DOK). Dr. Webb identified four levels for assessing the DOK of content standards and assessment items, stated below.

◆ *Level 1 (Recall)* includes the recall of information such as a fact, definition, term, or a simple procedure, as well as performing a simple algorithm or applying a formula. Key words that signify a Level 1 include "identify," "recall," "recognize," "use," and "measure."

◆ *Level 2 (Skill/Concept)* includes the engagement of some mental processing beyond a habitual response. A Level 2 assessment item requires students to make some decisions as to how to approach the problem. Keywords that generally distinguish a Level 2 include "classify," "organize," "estimate," "make observations," "collect and display data," and "compare data." These actions imply more than one step.

◆ *Level 3 (Strategic Thinking)* requires reasoning, planning, using evidence, and a higher level of thinking than the previous two levels. In most instances, requiring students to explain their thinking and make conjectures. The cognitive demands at Level 3 are complex and abstract. Level 3 activities include drawing conclusions from observations; citing evidence and developing a logical argument for concepts; and using concepts to solve problems.

◆ *Level 4 (Extended Thinking)* requires complex reasoning, planning, developing, and thinking most likely over an extended period of time. At Level 4, students should be required to make several connections—relate ideas *within* the content area or *among* content areas. Level 4 activities include designing and conducting experiments; making connections between a finding and related concepts and phenomena; combining and synthesizing ideas into new concepts; and critiquing experimental designs.

Traditional assessments can measure Level 1 and 2 standards with multiple-choice and short-response items, but performance tasks are often better suited to assess standards written at a Level 2 and beyond. Examining the verbs in the standards will provide teachers with important information on how cognitively demanding the assessment task needs to be.

In general, one should start small. Once the techniques and practices of performance assessment are well understood, and once teachers and students both have some experience in the methodology, performance tasks may be used frequently, particularly if they are small ones. However, when beginning, it is recommended that teachers use performance tasks infrequently, at a rate, for example, of four to six per year. Such a schedule permits teachers the time to create or adapt their tasks to ensure that they accomplish their desired purposes and to evaluate student work carefully. If only one or two tasks are administered per quarter, they should be those that are likely to reveal the most information about student understanding.

Once teachers have acquired experience in the use of performance tasks, they may want to use them more frequently and more informally. However, even with experience, few teachers will administer more than two or three such tasks per month.

Chapter Summary

◆ A curriculum map can be used to define which units or topics in a curriculum may be used to help students acquire the knowledge and skills inherent in a state's mathematics curriculum. The map is created by local educators, using their own curriculum, exercising professional judgment, to ensure that all the standards are being met comprehensively.

◆ Based on the curriculum map, educators can create an evaluation plan. This plan should include both traditional testing and performance assessment. As they move to performance assessment, teachers are advised to start small, with tasks that are written at a higher DOK level.

4

Understanding Quality Performance Tasks

Quality performance tasks are not simply something fun to do with one's students; they are not merely activities. While they may involve student activity, and they may be fun, they are highly purposeful. Performance tasks are designed to assess learning, and that fundamental purpose must remain foremost in the mind of anyone using them. The criteria for quality presented in this chapter will be essential as you consider adaptation and creation of performance tasks. These criteria center around three important interrelated questions:

- ◆ Does the task assess the content I want to assess?
- ◆ Does it meaningfully engage students?
- ◆ Does it provide a fair measurement of students' understanding?

The criteria that follow paint a picture of a quality performance task. A rubric that explicates each criterion and distinguishes between a quality performance task and one in need of improvement is included at the end of the chapter in Table 4.1.

Purpose

Any discussion of quality as it relates to performance tasks must necessarily begin with a clear understanding of assessment and the specific goals associated with performance assessment. In Chapter 2, we outline several benefits of performance assessment, including clarity as to criteria and standards, professional dialogue about criteria and standards, improved student work, high expectations, and student engagement.

A good performance task must assess what we want it to assess. It must, in other words, be aligned to the instructional goals we are interested in. Furthermore, the task should be designed in such a way that a student can complete the task correctly only by using the knowledge and skills being assessed.

We should never underestimate our students in this regard. While most students are not devious, most try to complete a task with as little risk and/or effort as possible. If they see an easy way to do the task, even by short-circuiting our intentions, they may well do it that way. Teachers should attempt, therefore, to create tasks that are as tight as possible, without being unduly rigid.

Additionally, while content standards have traditionally been front and center when developing assessment materials, standards-based reforms have provided us with a host of competencies, practices, and proficiencies that students should demonstrate as they engage in the kinds of open-ended problems that comprise performance tasks. Including an assessment of these practices takes advantage of the very nature of performance tasks. Excluding them from the assessment process would squander an opportunity to gather great evidence of student understanding.

☑ **Professional Development Tip**

Working with Colleagues to Align Content and Tasks

Engaging with colleagues is one way to deepen our understanding of the degree to which the task is tightly aligned to the identified content, often a standard or group of standards. In a collaborative teacher team meeting, begin by having all participants work out the task. Doing this has several benefits, including illustrating a variety of solution pathways. The opportunity to work with teachers from different grades (in K-5) can prove a valuable opportunity to collect a range of diverse responses to the task. You may wish to ask colleagues to respond to the task as if they were a student. Once the responses are generated, take time to closely analyze them. You may wish to refer to your state or district standards to identify the degree to which the responses to the task meet the demands of those standards. In doing so, you can better answer the question, "Does the task assess the content I want to assess?"

Engaging

Another critical feature of performance tasks is that they are engaging to students; it is essential that they be of interest and that students want to put forth their best effort. This suggests that the questions asked have intrinsic merit so that students don't read the question and respond, "So what?" or, "Who cares?" Engagement, as used here, refers to more than mere compliance, more than a student following a set of directions provided by the teacher. Here, we mean that quality performance tasks provide opportunities for students to think deeply and critically, to reason and construct mathematical arguments, and to make sense of problems that aren't merely an application of an algorithmic process already learned—and *ideally* to get students to want to do these things.

Engaging students in meaningful and purposeful work is one of the teacher's greatest challenges. But it's also a key goal to improving instruction and, ultimately, student achievement in mathematics. If we hold as a goal the preparation of students for an increasingly technological society that demands quantitative reasoning in both daily life and the world of work, we must commit to *engage* students in mathematics. Doing so also fosters students' engagement in a set of practices—variously referred to as habits of mind, mathematical processes, or mathematical practices—that have been at the center of mathematics reform for the better part of the past two decades.

Students are engaged when they study interesting or provocative questions. Often, these questions require students to construct arguments which, by their very nature, require rigorous mathematical thinking. For example, a task might require students to answer questions such as, "When subtracting, what happens to the minuend when the subtrahend decreases by 5? What happens when it increases by 5?" Elementary school students could answer these questions empirically by working through several examples. But it could also be proved algebraically and represented symbolically in middle school grades. In either case, these questions are puzzles, and puzzles are games, which generate student interest.

How does one find or create engaging tasks? As with so much else in education, professional judgment is the key. Successful instructional activities can be a good place to begin; most teachers know which activities, or which types of activities, are successful with their students. One of these activities, when adapted to the demands of assessment, might make a good performance task. And when reviewing tasks that others have created, one important criterion to always bear in mind is whether the task is likely to be engaging to students.

Authentic

Related to engagement is the issue of authenticity. Students tend to be more interested in those situations that resemble "real life" rather than those which are completely divorced from any practical application. This means that the task asks students to solve a realistic problem with clear and immediate applications in the real world. For instance, a task might require students to estimate how much money they'll need to pay for a basket of groceries as they study operations with decimals. Or it might require students to develop a scale model to assess their understanding of geometry and proportionality.

In addition, performance tasks that reflect the "messiness" of real life make demands on students that more sanitized situations do not. For example, real-life situations require that students make assumptions and identify constraints. Students can solve a system of linear equations in mathematics. Or, in a more authentic task, they might be asked to identify whether two different cell phone plans cost the same amount of money. Making a recommendation about the cheaper plan would require that students make assumptions about usage patterns. This is more like the decision an adult makes in the face of a cell phone marketplace that consists of many providers, different levels of call quality, and different pricing models. It is preferable to design or adapt performance tasks that represent authentic applications of knowledge and skill. This has the advantage of requiring students to use their knowledge and skill in much the same way it is used by adult practitioners in that field.

However, much of mathematics is highly formal and abstract and authenticity is not always possible. While teachers care that students can apply their mathematical knowledge to practical situations, there is much of mathematics, such as number theory, which is internal to the discipline. But such knowledge must be assessed, and a constructed-response question is preferable to a multiple-choice item. However, such a question will probably not reflect authentic application.

Enables Assessment of Individuals

Many performance tasks that sound imaginative are designed to be completed by students working in groups. And while such tasks may be valuable instructional activities and are certainly fun for the students, they cannot be used for the assessment of individuals. Assessment, after all, concerns the evaluation of individual learning; a performance task in which the contributions of different individuals are obscured cannot be used for such evaluation.

It is possible, of course, to design a performance task that includes both group and individual elements. For example, a group of students may be given some data and asked to analyze it. However, if the analysis is done as a group, each student should be required to produce an independent summary of what the data shows, and each individual's paper should be evaluated independently.

However, even in such a situation, the information for the teacher is somewhat compromised. When reading the work of an individual, a teacher knows only what that student could produce after having participated in a group with other students. With a different group of peers, that same student might have demonstrated much greater, or far less, understanding.

In general, then, it is preferable to create individual performance tasks if these are to be used solely for assessment purposes. If the goal also includes instructional purposes, then compromises on the individuality of the assessment tasks may be necessary.

Contains Clear Directions for Students

Any good performance task includes directions for students that are both complete and unambiguous. This is a fundamental principle of equity and good measurement. Students should never be in doubt about what it is they are to do on a performance task; the directions should be clear and complete. This does not preclude a task that includes the "messiness" described earlier, messiness that might require students to make assumptions when faced with incomplete data, for example. And it does not mean that the directions should be lengthy; on the contrary, shorter directions are preferable to longer ones.

Second, the directions should specifically ask students to do everything on which they will be evaluated. For example, if one of the assessment criteria for a mathematics problem involves the organization of information, students should be specifically instructed to "present their information in an organized manner," or some such wording.

Related to the question of directions is that of scaffolding, that is, how much support should students receive in accomplishing the performance task? For example, in a mathematics problem that involves a multi-step solution, should the students be prompted for each step, or is that part of the problem? The answer to this question relates to the purposes of the assessment, and the

Table 4.1 Performance Task Analytic Rubric

Element	In Need of Revision (Limited) (1)	Acceptable Task (2)	High Quality Task (3)
Engaging	◆ May be a problem similar to one already studied or of limited interest to students	◆ Some thought and persistence required to complete the task, though some aspects may only require application of previously learned procedures	◆ Provide students with a worthy question that requires thought and persistence to solve ◆ Task requires reasoning
Authentic	◆ Reflects a situation that wouldn't be encountered in the real world	◆ May reflect a situation that is similar to the real world, with parameters that make it somewhat artificial	◆ Reflects, to the degree possible, a real world application of the content targeted in the assessment
Clear	◆ Directions are unclear ◆ Evaluation criteria are not shared with students in advance of performance, either through a rubric or directions that specify the components of a satisfactory performance	◆ Directions are clear, but may not be sufficiently concise ◆ Evaluation criteria are partially shared with students, most likely through some direction regarding satisfactory performance or some rubric elements shared with students. May contain vague statements regarding evaluation, e.g., "students will be evaluated on presentation and clarity of work shown"	◆ Directions are clear and concise ◆ Evaluation criteria are shared clearly and precisely with students, e.g., through a rubric or directions which specify the components of a satisfactory performance
Elicits Desired Knowledge and Skill	◆ Task doesn't require that students have desired knowledge for successful completion	◆ Partially aligned to desired knowledge and skill, or may require other knowledge and skills (not a prerequisite of the desired knowledge and skills) to be successfully completed ◆ Includes opportunities in which students could demonstrate practices/"habits of mind," but doesn't require them to demonstrate satisfactory performance	◆ Aligned to relevant standards and curriculum ◆ Assesses mathematical content as well as practices/"habits of mind" ◆ Limits students' ability to demonstrate understandings other than those targeted with a correct and complete solution
Enables Assessment of Individuals	◆ The product is a result of group work in which one group member's contributions are indistinguishable from the contributions of other group members	◆ The product is a result of some group but also includes some work that is independently completed	◆ The task requires significant independent work, submitted independently of group work

age and skill level of the students. Less scaffolding is more authentic than more scaffolding; most problems are not presented to us with an outline of how to solve them. In general it is preferable to provide students with problems, with no scaffolding, that represent the optimal challenge for them to determine the proper approach on their own. An intermediate position is to present the problem, with no scaffolding, and then offer "tips" to the student to consider if desired. These tips can contain suggestions that, if followed, would provide guidance as to a possible approach to the problem.

Chapter Summary

◆ Good performance tasks share a number of important criteria. They elicit the desired knowledge and skill, meaningfully engage students, and fairly measure students' learning. These should be considered as tasks are designed and adapted.

◆ Engaging tasks are more than merely "interesting." They require reasoning and student engagement with a set of habits of mind/mathematical practices that reflect what successful mathematicians do.

5

Creating and Adapting
Performance Tasks

The evaluation plan that results from the analysis of curriculum outcomes and topics (determined in Chapter 3) provides the guidelines needed to actually design performance tasks. As part of that plan, educators will have decided which standards have a higher cognitive demand and Depth of Knowledge (DOK), or choose a cluster of standards that reflect the major work of the grade. Often standards that begin with the word "understand" are a good fit for a performance task.

In the design of performance tasks, a number of factors must be taken into consideration to achieve these ends. These are described in this chapter.

Size of Performance Tasks

Performance tasks may be large or small. Unique among assessment types, large tasks often take on many of the characteristics of instructional units in that students learn from engaging in the task. Large tasks, commonly referred to as projects, may require a week or more to complete. They are typically complex and authentic, and require students to synthesize information from many sources. Small tasks, on the other hand, are more like open-ended questions in which students solve a problem and explain their reasoning. These may be completed in a single class period or less. Naturally, there are a range of performance tasks that may be of medium length and complexity.

In deciding whether to use performance tasks that are large or small, educators must take a number of factors into account. These are outlined below.

Purpose

Teachers should be very clear about their purpose in using the performance task. What do they hope and plan to derive from it? Are their purposes purely those of assessment, or do they hope to accomplish some instructional purposes as well?

- ◆ *Small tasks are primarily suitable for purely assessment purposes.* If a teacher has taught a concept, and simply wants to know that students have understood that concept, then a small performance task is desirable. Such a task will ask students to solve a relatively small problem, to explain their thinking, and to show their work. However, it will not, in itself, also contain activities to be completed as part of the task. The task itself is designed primarily for assessment.
- ◆ *Large tasks carry instructional purposes as well as assessment ones.* Occasionally, a teacher will want students to truly learn new content as a result of completing an assessment task. If so, a larger task, spread over a number of days, involving many sub-activities, will accomplish this purpose better than a small task.
- ◆ *Culminating assessments require the assessments of a broader range of skills and conceptual understanding.* Large performance tasks are particularly well suited to culminating assessments because they tap a number of different types of skills and understandings. Smaller performance tasks can be combined to assess a larger instructional unit as a culminating assessment. However, if performance tasks are for the purpose of assessing a small part of the curriculum, small tasks are more useful since they can be administered frequently and the results used for adjusting instruction. The purpose of the assessment will be a major factor, then, in determining whether performance tasks should be large or small.

Curriculum Pressure and Time Demands

Generally speaking, when teachers are under pressure to "cover" many topics in the curriculum, and consequently have little time to spend on any one topic, they may find that small performance tasks are all that they have time for. Large tasks, while they include many benefits not derived from small ones, do require substantial amounts of time, frequently more than many teachers can devote to them. Indeed, small performance tasks are a great (and manageable) way for teachers to begin the use of performance assessment in their classrooms for a number of reasons:

◆ they are easier to construct or adapt from third party sources;
◆ they are easily administered in a short amount of time;
◆ they broaden the kinds of understandings that can be assessed.

Skill in Getting Started

Most educators, when they are just beginning to use performance tasks, are unsure of what they are doing; in such situations it is a good idea to use the "start small" principle. For example, when not sure whether the directions to students on a task are clear, it is better to discover that after the students have spent a class period, rather than a week, completing the task. Less time has been devoted to it and there may well be an opportunity to attempt another version of the same task, or a different task, later.

The Design Process

Now that your purpose for creating a performance task is clearly in mind, it is time to create one. What process should be followed? While there are several possible approaches, an effective one is described below.

Begin with a Clear Goal in Mind

As mentioned earlier in this chapter, a critical feature of a well-designed performance task is a clear alignment to the instructional goal(s) in which teachers are interested. In many cases, performance tasks will be designed to assess the major goals of an instructional unit. In that case, it is worth beginning by reviewing the standards and learning goals the author (whether a group of teachers or a curriculum publisher) of the instructional unit has identified. The size of the performance task and the instructional unit must be considered when determining "how much" the task will assess. It is problematic for a performance task to focus too narrowly on a skill or too broadly on too many concepts. With the development of the Common Core State Standards for Mathematics, it is important to attend to goals that reflect both the standards for mathematical content as well as the Standards for Mathematical Practice. In fact, performance tasks are uniquely positioned to provide teachers with assessments of students' mastery of the mathematical practices.

Create an Initial Design

With the specifications and criteria in mind, create an initial draft of a performance task to assess a given combination of student understanding and skill. This task may be created using the format provided in Figure 5.1 at the end of the chapter. This initial draft should be considered as just that, an initial draft—it will almost certainly be revised later in the process. A good way to begin the design process is to preview the vast number of performance tasks available online, in commercial programs, and in professional texts, such as this one, to get a sense of the style and type of task you'd like to develop. This is a critical step and should not be overlooked.

☑ **Professional Development Tip**

Designing Prototype Tasks

As a first step in designing performance tasks, consider gathering teachers at the same grade-level or who teach the same subject or course. Identify a set of standards, including both content standards and mathematical proficiencies/habits of mind, or a unit of study from your curriculum, and have each teacher generate a seed idea or prototype for a performance task designed to assess that content. Have each teacher type their prototype task or seed idea and place on posters in the room where the team meeting will take place.

Once the group is assembled, members should conduct a carousel walk, where appropriate, solving a prototype task or analyzing a seed idea. After cycling through all proposals, group members return to the poster at which they started and provide two pieces of feedback and one piece of advice, as follows:

◆ Identify a strength of the performance task prototype or idea and write on a sticky note to share. For example, you might notice that the task is well aligned to the content standards identified in the unit of study.

◆ Identify an area of growth or next step and share on a sticky note. For example, you might notice that the task could be solved using addition or multiplication, even though the unit is focused on multiplication.

◆ Last, share a recommendation on how to improve the task. For example, you might suggest that the task include directions to students to show their work to enable better assessment of conceptual understanding.

At the end of this exercise, your team will have several possible seed ideas that can be adapted, developed, merged or discarded. In any case, you'll have harnessed the power of collective thinking to begin the process of drafting a performance task.

Figure 5.1 Performance Task Design Worksheet

Task title: _____

Course:

Unit or topic:

Standard(s) addressed:

Brief description of the task (what students must do, and what product will result):
(For short performance tasks, include problem here.)

Directions to the students:

Criteria to be used to evaluate student responses:

EXAMPLE

Task title: *Ocean Math Story*

Course: *Math Third Quarter*

Unit or topic: *Word Problems, Operations & Algebraic Thinking*

Standard(s) addressed:

CCSS.MATH.CONTENT.1.OA.A.1: *Use addition and subtraction within 20 to solve word problems involving situations of adding to, taking from, putting together, taking apart, and comparing, with unknowns in all positions, e.g., by using objects, drawings, and equations with a symbol for the unknown number to represent the problem.*

Brief description of the task (what students must do, and what product will result):
(For short performance tasks, include problem here.)

Students will write and solve their own word problem, within 20.

Directions to the students:

Use the Ocean Storyboard and the ocean animals to create your own math story. Write a story about your picture. Ask us a math question and give us enough information to solve the problem. Then on another piece of paper, solve your problem and write an equation to show the answer.

Criteria to be used to evaluate student responses:

◆ *Written problem, including question, shows an understanding of addition or subtraction as an operation, within 20.*
◆ *Illustration (picture or drawings) reflects one of the word problem types and can be used to solve the problem.*
◆ *Solution is accurate and equation demonstrates an understanding of the unknown.*

Obtain Colleague Review

If possible, persuade one or more colleagues to review your work. These may be teachers who work in the same discipline as you or with the same age students, or they may be teachers with very different responsibilities. Both approaches have their advantages and their drawbacks.

Teachers with different responsibilities are more likely to catch ambiguity or lack of clarity in the directions to students than are teachers who are as expert in the field as you are. On the other hand, expert colleagues are better able to provide feedback on the content being addressed in the task and spot situations in which it is not completely valid; that is, situations in which students would be able to complete the task successfully without the desired knowledge and skill. Therefore, a colleague review that includes a combination of content experts and non-experts is ideal.

Pilot Task with Students

Not until a performance task is tried with students is it possible to know whether it can accomplish its desired purpose. Only then can teachers know whether the directions are clear, whether all elements are properly requested, and whether the task truly elicits the desired knowledge and skill. Careful attention should be paid to the verbs in the standards themselves, to determine whether the child is able to demonstrate a complete or fragile understanding of the concepts.

Piloting with students is also the only way to know the degree to which the task is engaging and accessible to them. Students are likely to be honest in their reaction to a performance task, perhaps more honest than their teachers would like. While it is possible to collect their feedback formally, it is generally evident from their level of engagement and from the quality of their responses whether the task is a good one or not, or how it could be improved.

Revise Performance Task

As a result of the colleague review and the pilot with students, the draft task will, no doubt, require some revision. This revision might be a major rewrite or it might be a minor "tweak" in order to make the task clearer, less cumbersome, or differently slanted.

Once revised, the task is ready for the formal process of rubric design discussed in Chapter 7. However, teachers should be aware that the task may need further revision after the scoring rubric is written—that exercise frequently reveals inadequacies (usually minor) in the task itself.

Adapting Existing Performance Tasks

Often, you can save time and effort by adapting an existing task for your own use. Many state departments of education have created prototype tasks, and textbook publishers often offer tasks as part of their package.

Matching Outcomes, Topics, and Students

The first step in identifying tasks suitable for adaptation is to match the outcomes and topics assessed by the task with those in one's own curriculum. The performance tasks in this book have been aligned with the Common Core State Standards. By examining those alignments, educators can determine whether a given task would be of value to them in assessing student mastery of their own curriculum.

It is unlikely that such a match will be perfect. Frequently, a performance task will ask students to perform an operation or complete an activity that students in a given class have not yet learned. Even tasks well aligned to the Common Core State Standards may not be well aligned to the scope and sequence of topics addressed in a particular curriculum or with a particular group of students. Alternatively, a scoring rubric will include criteria that do not reflect a district's curriculum or priorities. In those cases, either the task or the rubric will have to be adjusted.

Chapter Summary

◆ The size of a performance task is best determined by its purpose (immediate or culminating assessment, or instruction) and by the time constraints and experience of the teacher. In general, it is recommended that teachers begin their efforts with performance assessment using tasks which are small rather than large. This provides the opportunity to experiment with a new methodology in a way that carries low stakes for success, for both the students and the teacher.

◆ The process of task design has several steps, all of which should be completed. A performance task should not be used for actual assessment until it has been piloted with students. This suggests that at least a year will elapse between the decision to embark on a program of performance assessment and the implementation of such a system.

◆ In order to determine whether an existing performance task can be used as written, educators must match the task's outcomes and topics with those in their curriculum, and consider their own students.

6

Using Rubrics to Evaluate Complex Performance

A Nonschool Example

All of the principles involved in the evaluation of complex performance may be illustrated by an everyday example—going to a restaurant. Reading through this example readers address, in a more familiar form, all of the issues that they encounter in designing systems of performance assessment for classroom use. Moreover, it becomes evident that the methods for evaluating performance reflect, at their heart, only common sense.

The Situation

Imagine that we are opening a restaurant in your town and that we are now ready to hire servers. We know that it is important that the servers be skilled, so we want to hire the best that we can find. As part of our search, we have decided to eat in some existing restaurants to see if there are people working in these establishments that we can lure to our restaurant. Consequently, we are preparing to embark on our search mission.

The Criteria

How will we know what to look for? We must determine the five or six most important qualities we would watch for in a good server. But because our focus is on "performance," we should list only those qualities that are visible to a customer (such as appearance), and not other qualities which, while they might be important to an employer (such as getting to work on time), are not seen by a customer.

A reasonable list of criteria includes such qualities as courtesy, appearance, responsiveness, knowledge, coordination, and accuracy. It is important to write the criteria using neutral rather than positive words. That is, for reasons that will become apparent shortly, we should write "appearance" rather than "neat."

These criteria could, of course, become a checklist. That is, we could eat in a restaurant and determine whether our server was courteous, or responsive, or knowledgeable, and so forth. We could answer each of the items with a "yes" or "no," and then count the "yeses." However, life tends to be more complex than a checklist—a server might be *somewhat* knowledgeable, *mostly* accurate, *a little bit* coordinated.

How do we accommodate these degrees of performance? How do we design a system that respects the complexity of the performance, yet that allows us to compare two or more individuals. The answer is to create a rubric, a scoring guide.

The Scoring Guide or Rubric

Table 6.1 is a rubric, which is simply a guide for evaluating performance.

Table 6.1 Server Evaluation Rubric

	Level One	Level Two	Level Three	Level Four
Courtesy				
Appearance				
Responsiveness				
Knowledge				
Coordination				
Accuracy				

The criteria that are important for servers in our fledgling restaurant are listed in the left column. Across the top, are columns for different levels of performance. In this case, there are four levels. The double-line between Levels Two and Three indicates that performance at Levels Three and Four is acceptable, but performance at Levels One and Two is unacceptable. We could, then, broadly define the different levels as:

Level One: unacceptable
Level Two: almost, but not quite, good enough
Level Three: acceptable
Level Four: exemplary

In each box, then, we would write descriptions of actual performance that would represent each level for each criterion. For example, for "coordination" we might decide that an individual at Level One is someone who actually spilled an entire bowl of soup, or a cup of coffee, or who could not handle a tray of dishes; an individual at Level Two is someone who spilled a little coffee in the saucer, or who spilled some water while filling the glasses; a person at Level Three is someone who spilled nothing; and a person at Level Four is someone who balanced many items without mishap.

We could fill in the entire chart with such descriptions, and we would then be ready to go evaluate prospective employees. A possible profile might look like Table 6.2:

Table 6.2 A Completed Server Rubric

Name: Jamie Jones   **Restaurant: Hilltop Cafe**

	Level One	Level Two	Level Three	Level Four
Courtesy		X		
Appearance				X
Responsiveness			X	
Knowledge	X			
Coordination				X
Accuracy			X	

We still have to decide, of course, whether to hire this individual, or whether this individual was preferable to another candidate whose scores were all "3s." That is, we still have to determine how to arrive at a composite score for each individual so that we can compare them.

If we were using this approach for supervision or coaching rather than for hiring, we would not need to combine scores on the different criteria. We could use the scores for feedback and coaching. For example, because this individual is, apparently, not very knowledgeable, we could provide assistance in that area. We could then work on courtesy, and make sure that customers feel comfortable around this person. That is, for supervision or coaching purposes, the system is diagnostic and enables us to provide specific and substantive feedback on areas needing improvement.

Measurement and Practical Issues

When we contemplate applying these principles to the evaluation of student performance, we encounter a number of issues which, while not technically complex, must be addressed before this approach can be implemented. It should be borne in mind that most teachers have rubrics in their minds for student performance; they apply these every time they grade a student's paper. However, communication is vastly improved if educators can be explicit about the criteria they use in evaluating student work and about what their expectations are. Achieving this clarity requires the teacher to address a number of technical and practical issues.

The Number and Type of Criteria

For a given performance, how many criteria should we have? For example, when evaluating a persuasive essay, how many different things should we look for? Should we evaluate organization separately from structure? What about the use of language or, specifically, the use of vocabulary; or correct spelling and mechanics? What about sentence structure and organization? Should we consider the essay's impact on us, the reader? Is it important that we be persuaded by the argument?

Clearly, some of these elements are related to one another: it would be difficult, in a persuasive essay, for example, to have good use of language independently of the vocabulary used. However, other criteria are completely separate from one another. A student's inadequacies in mechanics and spelling, for example, will not affect the persuasiveness of the argument, unless it is so poor as to hinder communication.

The number of criteria used should reflect, insofar as is possible, those aspects of performance that are simultaneously important and independent of one another. With primary students, three or four criteria that demonstrate organization and approach, mathematical accuracy, and oral or written presentations are appropriate. The criteria should reflect the age and skill of the students. With young children or students with special needs, for example, it might be necessary to identify specific aspects of punctuation that are evaluated—proper use of capital letters, commas, and semicolons—whereas for high school students these may all be clustered under "punctuation" and can include all aspects of mechanics.

However, when criteria are clustered in such a way that they include several elements, these should be specifically identified. Just as "appearance" in the server example might include the person's uniform, condition of the hair and nails, and general grooming, individual criteria should specify what elements are included. For example, "use of language" might include richness of vocabulary, use of persuasive words, and proper use of specialized terms.

Moreover, the criteria should reflect those aspects of performance that are truly most important, not merely those that are easiest to see or count. Thus, a rubric for writing should include more than spelling and mechanics; a rubric for problem solving should include criteria dealing with the student's thought processes, the use of models and strategies.

A rubric should not include so many criteria that it is difficult to use. On the other hand, it should include every element considered important. As a general rule, because most people cannot hold more than five or six items in their mind simultaneously, rubrics should not contain more than five or six criteria. The ones in this book generally have 3–4 criteria.

Analytic vs. Holistic Rubrics

The server rubric developed in the previous section is an example of an *analytic* rubric, that is, different criteria are identified and levels of performance are described for each. A similar rubric, but with different criteria defined and described, is usable in the classroom to *analyze* the strengths and weaknesses of student work.

With a *holistic* rubric, on the other hand, the features of performance on all criteria for a given score are combined so that it is possible, for example, to describe a "Level Two" or a "Level Four" server. Such holistic judgments are necessary when a single score, such as on an advanced placement test, must be given. However, compromises are necessary, because an individual piece of work usually does not include all the features of a certain level. Therefore, analytic rubrics are recommended for classroom use, because they provide much more complete information for feedback to students.

How Many Points on the Scale?

In the server example, we identified four points on the scale. That was an arbitrary decision; we could have selected more or less. Performance on any criterion, after all, falls along a continuum; designating points on a scale represents, to some degree, a compromise between practical demands and the complexity of real performance. However, in deciding on the number of points to use, there are several important considerations to remember:

- ◆ *Fineness of distinctions.* More points offer the opportunity to make very fine distinctions between levels of performance. However, scales with many points are time-consuming to use because the differences between the points are likely to be small.
- ◆ *Even vs. odd.* In general, an even number of points is preferable to an odd number. This relates to the measurement principle of central tendency, which states that many people, if given the opportunity, will assign a score in the middle of a range. If there is no middle, as on a scale with an even number of points, they are required to make a commitment to one side or the other.

However, these considerations apply to rubrics that are constructed for application to a single activity or type of performance. For *developmental* rubrics, a large number of points may be preferable. In a developmental rubric, students' performance over an extended period of time with respect to important concepts and skills is monitored on a single rubric. Such rubrics are representative of learning progressions in which understanding ranges from a rudimentary level to an advanced level in a single domain. For example, the proportional reasoning learning progression developed by Baxter and Junker ranges from an intuitive understanding of at which students can answer questions about fairness to a level at which students have a generalized model for solving proportionality problems and a repertoire of solution strategies. A student in early elementary school may have an intuitive understanding of proportional reasoning but may not have a generalized model for solving problems involving proportionality until they are in middle or high school. For example, the Number and Operations progressions developed by the Common Core writing team, highlight the development that takes place as students grapple with 1–1 correspondence, cardinality, counting all, counting on, and using derived facts to add and subtract. Later they apply the commutative and associative properties of operations to efficiently solve for multi-digit combinations. A developmental rubric with many points on the scale is extremely useful in proportional reasoning and in other domains because it can be used to chart a student's progress with respect to important concepts and skills over an extended period of time providing an informed direction for instruction that moves students to the next level in a learning progression.

Dividing Line between Acceptable and Unacceptable Performance

It is important to decide, at the outset, where the line will be between acceptable and unacceptable performance. A dichotomous sort (good enough/not good enough) forces teachers to determine what work is proficient. This activity is at the heart of setting a standard because teachers thereby communicate, to their colleagues as well as to their students, the quality of work they expect.

In the server example, the line between acceptable and unacceptable performance was established between Levels Two and Three. This, too, is arbitrary; it could just as well been put between Levels One and Two. When determining where to place the dividing line, educators should consider several points:

- ◆ *Use.* If a scoring rubric is to be used for formative evaluation, it is helpful to identify several levels of unacceptable performance so that teachers can know quickly whether a student's performance on a certain criterion is close to being acceptable, or is far away. Such knowledge can guide further instruction. On the other hand, if a rubric is to be used to make a summative judgment only, then it is less important whether a student's performance is close to the cut-off point; unacceptable is unacceptable, without regard to degrees of unacceptability.

- ◆ *Number of points on the scale.* If a scoring rubric is constructed with six, seven, or eight points, then the placement of the "unacceptable" line might be different than for a rubric with only four points. A five-point scale (while not ideal from the standpoint of having an odd number of points) allows two levels of unacceptable while also permitting finer degrees of excellence, with the upper levels representing, for example, barely acceptable, good, and excellent.

- ◆ *Developmental vs. non-developmental rubrics.* Clearly, for a developmental rubric that defines performance over an extended period of time, there is no need to define the distinction between acceptable and unacceptable performance in the same manner as for a performance-specific rubric. In this case, judgments as to acceptability and expectations do not reside in the rubric, but in the use that is made of them in different settings.

Titles for Levels of Performance

Closely related to the need to define the cut-off between acceptable and unacceptable performance is the requirement to broadly define the labels for each point on the rubric. Teachers often use words such as "unacceptable" and "exemplary." Although such descriptions might work even if students (or their families) will see the rubric, such descriptions should be given some thought. Some educators prefer designations like "novice," "emerging," "proficient," and "distinguished." Decisions as to the best headings are matters for professional judgment and consensus. Naturally, it's possible to simply use numbers (1, 2, 3, etc.) without implying judgment.

Descriptions of Performance

Descriptions for levels of performance should be written in language that is truly descriptive rather than comparative. For example, words such as "average" should be avoided, as in "the number of computational errors is average," and replaced by statements such as "the solution contains only minor computational errors." "Minor" will then have to be defined, as, for example, "an error not resulting in an erroneous conclusion," or "an error that was clearly based in carelessness." In this case, it's not the number of errors but the type of mistakes that make a difference in the level of performance.

Generic vs. Task-Specific

Constructing a performance rubric for student work takes considerable time, particularly if it is a joint effort among many educators. The issue of time, and the desire to send a consistent signal to students and their families regarding standards, are important reasons to try to create generic rubrics. Such rubrics may be used for many different specific tasks that students do.

The areas of student performance that appear to lend themselves best to generic rubrics are such things as math journals, problem solving tasks, expository (or descriptive, or argument) essays, and oral presentations. Some of these, for example, oral presentations, are suitable for several different disciplines. It is highly valuable for students to know, in a consistent manner, that when they are preparing an oral presentation, it will always be evaluated, in every situation, and in every course at the secondary level, using the same criteria.

However, generic rubrics are not always possible, or even desirable. The elements of problem solving, and certainly the levels of acceptable performance, are very different for high school sophomores than for second graders. So while there are many reasons to construct rubrics that are as generic as possible—intra- and cross-departmental discussions are highly recommended—it may not be possible to develop completely generic rubrics, There are many types of tasks that require their own, task-specific rubric.

Professional Consensus

When teachers work together to determine descriptions of levels of performance in a scoring rubric, they may find that they do not completely agree. This is natural and to be expected. After all, it is well-documented that teachers grade student work quite differently from one another.

Discussions about the proper wording for different levels of performance constitute rich professional experiences. While difficult, the discussions are generally enriching for everyone involved; most teachers find that their ideas can be enhanced by the contributions of their colleagues. Rubrics that are the product of many minds are generally superior to those created by individuals. In addition, if a number of teachers find that they can use the same, or similar, rubrics for evaluating student work, communication with students is that much more consistent, resulting in better quality work from students.

Inter-Rater Agreement

Closely related to reaching consensus on the descriptions of performance levels is the matter of agreement on the rubric's application. The only way to be sure that there is agreement on the meaning of the descriptions of different levels is to apply the statements to samples of student work.

The importance of this issue cannot be emphasized enough. It is a fundamental principle of equity and fairness that evaluation of a student's work be the same regardless of who is doing the evaluating. However, teachers rarely agree completely at the beginning. Occasionally, two teachers will evaluate a single piece of student work very differently, even when they have agreed on the scoring rubric. In those cases, they generally discover that they were interpreting words in the rubric differently, or that the words used were themselves ambiguous. Only by trying the rubric with actual student work are such difficulties revealed.

When preparing rubrics for evaluating student work, therefore, the project is not totally complete until examples of different levels of performance are selected to illustrate the points on the scale. Called "anchor papers," these samples serve to maintain consistency in scoring.

Clarity of Directions

Another fundamental principle of fairness and equity concerns the directions given to students. Any criterion to be evaluated must be clearly asked for in the directions to a performance task. For example, if students are to be evaluated on their originality in making an oral presentation, something in the directions to them should recommend that they present it in an original or creative manner. Likewise, if students are to be evaluated on the organization of their data, they should know that organization is important. Otherwise, from a student's point of view, it is necessary to read the teacher's mind to guess what is important.

Some teachers even find that they can engage students in the development of the rubric itself. Students, they discover, know the indicators of a good oral presentation or of a well-solved problem. While students' thoughts are rarely well-enough organized to enable them to create a rubric on their own, their ideas make good additions to a teacher-drafted rubric.

There are many advantages to engaging students in the construction of a scoring rubric. Most obviously, they know what is included and can, therefore, focus their work. But even more importantly, students tend to do better work, with greater pride in it and with greater attention to its quality, when the evaluation criteria are clear. Suddenly, school is not a matter of "gotcha," it is a place where excellent work is both defined and expected.

Combining Scores on Criteria

Occasionally, it is important to combine scores on different criteria and to arrive at a single evaluation. For example, teachers must occasionally rank students, or convert their judgments on performance to a grade or to a percentage. How can this be done?

In arriving at a single, holistic score, several issues must be addressed:

◆ *Weight*. Are all the criteria of equal importance? Unless one or another is designated as more or less important than the others, they should all be assumed to be of equal importance. Educators should have good reasons for their decisions as to weight, and these discussions can themselves constitute important professional conversations. As an example, when creating the server rubric, we could have determined that "knowledge" is the most important criterion and that it is worth twice the value of the others. Then, our rubric, and the points possible from each point, would appear as shown in Table 6.3.

◆ *Calculations*. How should the scores be calculated? Clearly, the easiest technique is to convert the assigned scores on each criterion, as reflected in the weights assigned to each criterion, to a percentage of the total possible number of points, using a formula similar to this:

Score Assigned × Weight = Criterion Score
Criterion Score on Each Criterion = Total Score
Total Score/Total Possible Scores = Percentage Score

Table 6.3 Weighted Server Rubric

Name: Jamie Jones   Restaurant: Hilltop Cafe

	Level One	Level Two	Level Three	Level Four
Courtesy Weight = 1		X		
Appearance Weight = 1				X

(continued)

Table 6.3 *(continued)*

	Level One	Level Two	Level Three	Level Four
Responsiveness Weight = 1			X	
Knowledge Weight = 2	X			
Coordination Weight = 1				X
Accuracy Weight = 1			X	

Using this procedure for Jamie Jones, her point score is:

Courtesy:	2 (2 × 1)
Appearance:	4 (4 × 1)
Responsiveness:	3 (3 × 1)
Knowledge:	2 (1 × 2)
Coordination:	4 (4 × 1)
Accuracy:	3 (3 × 1)
Total:	18

On this rubric, the maximum possible score for each criterion is:

Courtesy:	4
Appearance:	4
Responsiveness:	4
Knowledge:	8
Responsiveness:	4
Accuracy:	4
Total:	28

Thus, in our example, Jamie Jones received a score of 18 which, when divided by 28, is 64%.

◆ *Cut score.* What is the overall level of acceptable performance? We defined earlier the line between acceptable and unacceptable performance for each criterion. However, we must now determine a score which, overall, represents acceptable performance. We could set it as a percentage, for example 70%, in which case Jamie Jones would not be hired in our restaurant. Alternatively, we could establish a rule that no more than one criterion may be rated below three. This decision, like all the others made in constructing a performance rubric, is a matter of professional judgment.

Time

Not only for large-scale assessment, but also in the classroom, teachers know that multiple choice, short-answer, matching, and true/false tests take far less time to score than essay or open-ended tests. It is a relatively simple matter to take a stack of student tests and grade them against an answer key. Many educators fear that using performance tasks and rubrics will consume more time than they have or want to devote to it.

There is some validity to this concern. It is true that the evaluation of student work using a rubric takes more time than does grading student tests against a key. And the rubric itself can take considerable time to create.

However, there are two important issues to consider. One relates to the increasing ease of using performance tasks, and the second relates to the benefits derived from their use.

◆ *Decreasing time demands.* When they are just beginning to use performance tasks and rubrics, many teachers find that the time requirements are far greater than those needed for traditional tests. However, as they become more skilled, and as the rubrics they have developed prove to be useful for other assignments or other types of work, teachers discover that they can evaluate student work efficiently and, in many cases, in very little more time, if any, than that required for traditional tests.

◆ *Other benefits.* Most teachers discover that the benefits derived from increased use of performance tasks and rubrics vastly outweigh the additional time needed. They discover that students produce better quality work and that students take greater pride in that work. When performance tasks and rubrics are used as a component in assigning grades, teachers find that they can justify their decisions far more reliably than before they used rubrics.

Subjectivity vs. Objectivity

An important reservation about the use of rubrics to evaluate student work concerns their perceived "subjectivity" when compared to the "objectivity" of multiple-choice tests. Such fears, while understandable, are unjustified.

First, it is important to remember that the only objective feature to a multiple-choice test is its scoring; answers are unambiguously right or wrong. However, many professional judgments have entered into making the test itself, and even into determining which of the possible answers is the correct one. Someone must decide what questions to ask and how to structure the problems. These decisions reflect a vision of what are the important knowledge and skill for students to demonstrate, and are based on professional judgment.

Similarly, in the construction of a scoring rubric, many decisions must be made. These, too, are made on the basis of professional judgment. But the fact that they are made by teachers in their classrooms, rather than by testing companies, does not make them less valid judgments. It may be argued that, if well thought out, such judgments are superior to those made by anonymous agencies far from the realities of one's own classroom.

In any event, both scoring rubrics to evaluate student work and standardized tests are grounded in professional judgment. They are absolutely equivalent on that score. In both cases, it is the quality of the judgments that is important, and the classroom-based judgment may be as good as that made by the testing company.

Chapter Summary

◆ Rubrics are complex and rigorous tools for evaluating complex performance.

◆ Rubrics of high quality are a result of many factors, including the appropriateness of the number and titles of levels or performance, the match between the type of rubric bring used to the performance being evaluated, and the dividing line between acceptable and unacceptable performance.

◆ Analytic rubrics can be used to evaluate student work on multiple, independent criteria. However, they can also be used to generate holistic scores of student work. Generating holistic scores with rubrics sometimes requires weighting to ensure more important components of performance factor more heavily into a final score.

☑ **Professional Development Tip**

Analyzing Rubrics

One way to begin to familiarize yourself with rubrics is to engage in an analysis of several examples. A mix of quality, vetted rubrics and those that result from an internet search can provide a good supply to begin the review. A good place to begin collect rubrics is your state department of education. Generally, they publish samples of rubrics used to evaluate work from end-of-course or annual examinations. These are good to use as a reference, as they also reflect the standard to which students' work is held on these examinations. Additionally, curriculum publishers often include a variety of generic and specific rubrics to which you should refer in your search.

Each participant in the session should receive several sample rubrics (preferably without the source information included), and should analyze the following aspects of each rubric:

◆ What criteria does the rubric measure? Are some criteria more heavily weighted than others in a scoring formula?

◆ How many performance levels are there? (Are there an odd or even number?) What are they titled? Do they use supportive, positive titles for each performance level?

◆ Where is the dividing line between acceptable and unacceptable performance?

◆ Is this a generic or task-specific rubric? Is it a holistic, analytic or developmental rubric?

◆ Is the language used in the rubric clear? Does it require further definition/explanation (e.g., the "minor" error example above)?

Reviewing the rubrics for these elements can help familiarize participating teachers with elements that are useful for judging quality. Additional review can focus on the elements of the rubric that are useful when evaluating student work. Professional conversations about the utility of the rubric as well as the elements of performance evaluated by the rubric can be invaluable as teachers refine their understanding of the types of rubrics and criteria for judging their quality.

7

Creating and Adapting Rubrics

Developing a rubric is no small feat. With experience—teaching the same grade level or course over the course of several years, for instance—teachers come to understand how students' understandings develop and the common errors and misconceptions that may be exhibited in students' work. However, it is easy to underestimate the challenge of identifying what students must show in their work to be considered proficient. Similarly, there are many ways in which students can fall short of the proficient bar. The development of the task and the application of the rubric should be considered an iterative process (as each is developed and used, it suggests changes in the other) with the final combination of task and rubric evolving over time. This section includes guidance for the design of a rubric for a task.

Drafting a Scoring Rubric

Generally speaking, the criteria to be used in evaluating student work will have been identified in the course of developing a performance task. They should reflect the standards and learning goals being assessed by the performance task. However, in order to convert these criteria into an actual scoring rubric, they must be elaborated and further defined. As described in Chapter 6, there are two main types of rubrics, holistic and analytic. Holistic rubrics are designed to capture the overall quality of a student's performance on the task. Analytic rubrics, on the other hand, break down performance into multiple dimensions.

Each dimension is then elaborated and defined across multiple levels of performance. While holistic rubrics have their uses (e.g., in the summative evaluation of student work for awarding a diploma), this section will focus on the design of analytic rubrics.

Generic or Task-Specific?

The first question to be answered concerns the degree of task-specificity of the rubric. If, for example, the rubric is being developed for a group mathematics project, could the same rubric be used for other projects, or is its use confined to this particular one? Indeed, could the elements of the rubric, concerned with making a group presentation, be used for other disciplines as well? Are there enough similarities between group presentations for mathematics, science, and social studies that the same evaluation guide could be used for all of them? In addition to the application to different types of performances (e.g., individual versus group), different disciplines, generic rubrics can be most valuable when applied across performances as a tool for assessing students' growth. For example, a generic rubric could be used to assess students' ability to solve multistep addition and subtraction word problems across a school year (or multiple school years).

Table 7.1 Performance Rubric (Activity)

Criteria	1	2	3	4

In general, of course, generic rubrics are more useful that task-specific ones. Creating rubrics is time-consuming and the more broadly they may be applied, the more useful and powerful they are. However, sometimes a generic rubric will have to be adapted when the ways in which elements appear in student work are sufficiently different to warrant independent consideration.

Task- or Genre-Specific, or Developmental?

Another important question to be considered when creating a rubric is whether the rubric will be used on a single task (or a single type of task) or whether it will be used developmentally with students as they progress through many years of school. That is, will the rubric under development for a mathematics project be applied for only this particular project which students do in the fourth grade, or could it be used also with students throughout the district, including those in the middle school as well as in high school?

If the rubric is to be used developmentally, it will probably have many more points on its scale, and the criteria may be written differently than if the rubric is to be used for a single task. A developmental rubric is useful for a school in which students have mathematics portfolios, and may be helpful in charting progress over time. However, a developmental rubric may not be as useful for any particular task as one created specifically for that task.

Determining Criteria

Once the question of whether to develop a task-specific or generic rubric has been answered, the most important single step in creating a scoring rubric is to identify the criteria to be evaluated. The importance of attending carefully to this step cannot be overstated. It is in the determination of criteria that educators define important aspects of performance, and define, both for themselves and their students, what they mean by good quality. When defining criteria, several issues should be considered.

- ◆ *Type of criteria.* In mathematics, an essential criterion almost always concerns mathematical accuracy. Is the answer correct? Are computational errors major or minor? Are answers correctly labeled? Are all possible answers found?

    But in addition to computational accuracy, what else is important? What about conceptual understanding? Do students reveal, either through their approach to the problem or through the errors they make, that they have good understanding of the underlying concepts? Does the problem require a plan? If so, have students organized their information? Have they approached the problem in a systematic manner? Can a reader follow the student's line of reasoning?

    In addition, a mathematics project might require that students collaborate with one another. How successfully do they do this? Do they establish an equitable division of labor, or do one or two students dominate the group? If the students make a presentation as part of the project, do they explain their thinking clearly? Are the other students interested in the presentation? Can they follow it? Is it engaging? It is important that the criteria identified for a task not consist only of those that are easiest to see, such as computational accuracy. The criteria should, taken together, define all the aspects of exemplary performance, even if some of them are somewhat challenging to specify and to evaluate.

One successful approach to the identification of criteria is to consider the task and to imagine an excellent student response to it. What would such a response include? The answer to that question can serve to identify important criteria. It is recommended that teachers do the task themselves prior to assigning it to their students, creating, in effect, an exemplary response, and appreciating the issues inherent in the task for students.

◆ *Number and detail of criteria.* There is no single best answer to the question of "how many criteria?" Clearly, all important aspects of performance should be captured in the criteria. Moreover, those aspects of performance that are independent of one another should be designated as separate criteria.

It is possible to designate too many criteria, and for them to be too detailed. The resulting rubric is then cumbersome and time-consuming to use. On the other hand, a rubric that is too economical may not provide adequate information to students for them to improve performance or for teachers to use in helping students improve. The number and level of detail of the rubric then, is partly a matter of how it is to be used and the age and skill level of the students. Rubrics used with students with special needs, for example, are often made in great detail, so both teachers and students are aware of where improvement efforts should be focused.

◆ *Sub-criteria or elements.* Sometimes, several criteria are related to one another or one may be considered a sub-category of another. In that case, the criteria may contain within them sub-criteria or elements. For example, if students make a presentation as part of the mathematics project, the overall criterion might be "quality of presentation" with sub-criteria of "clarity," "originality and energy," and "involvement of all group members."

Occasionally, when educators think critically about the qualities they would look for in good student performance, they recognize that the task, as written, does not elicit those qualities; they then return to the task and alter the student directions. That is, students could do the task and not demonstrate the criteria that have been defined. In that case, the directions must be rewritten, or the task restructured, to elicit the desired performance.

Number of Points

Critical to the design of rubrics in the number of points used to evaluate each criterion. One important design consideration not to be overlooked: as mentioned in Chapter 6, an even number is preferable to an odd number, since it prevents the phenomenon known as "central tendency." But beyond that, there are several considerations to keep in mind.

- ◆ *Detail in distinctions.* With a larger number of points on a scale, fine distinctions are required when evaluating student work. While such detail can provide finely-tuned feedback to students and information for teachers, a rubric with many points is difficult to write and cumbersome and time-consuming to use. For practical purposes, a rubric with 4–6 points is recommended. The tasks in this collection all contain 4 points.
- ◆ *Dividing line between acceptable and unacceptable performance.* It is helpful, at the outset, to determine the dividing line between acceptable and unacceptable performance. On a 4-point scale, this line is either between the "1" and the "2" or between the "2" and the "3." That placement will be determined by where the greater detail is the more useful; that is, is it more useful to be able to specify degrees of inadequacy or degrees of adequacy?
- ◆ *General headings for different points.* The different points on the scale may be called simply by their numbers. On a 4-point scale then, they would be 0, 1, 2, and 3 or 1, 2, 3, and 4. Or, they could be 10, 20, 30, and 40. Alternatively, the points can be given names such as "novice," "emerging," "proficient," and "exemplary." If this approach is taken, it is preferable to use positive, supportive words (such as "emerging") rather than negative ones (such as "inadequate").

Descriptions of Levels of Performance

Once the criteria and the number of scale points have been determined, it is time to actually write the descriptions of performance levels. Again, this step is critical and includes a number of factors.

- ◆ *The language used.* The words used to specify the qualities of different levels of performance should be descriptive, rather than comparative. For example, words such as "average" should be avoided. The descriptions of performance levels serve to further define the criteria, and are further defined themselves only when accompanied by actual samples of student work, called anchor papers. When describing the qualities of lower levels of performance, it is important to include elements that will exist in the work alongside things that are missing. So, for example, rather than defining emerging performance as merely, "unable to solve multistep word problems involving addition and subtraction," a rubric would better serve its users if it defined emerging performance as, "able to solve single-step word problems involving addition and subtraction."

◆ *All sub-criteria or elements defined.* If the criteria contain sub-criteria within them, each of these elements should be described in each of the performance descriptions. For example, if a criterion on presentation includes accuracy and originality, and involvement of all group members, then the descriptions for each of the levels should describe the group's presentation with respect to all those elements. This parallel rubric structure enables teachers to more easily evaluate performance on sub-criteria and provide clear feedback to students.

◆ *Distance between points.* To the extent possible, the distance between the points on a scale should be equal. That is, the distance between a "3" and a "4" should not be much greater than that between a "2" and a "3."

◆ *Defining proficiency.* Placement of the line between acceptable (proficient) and unacceptable performance should receive particular scrutiny. While the highest and lowest levels of performance are the easiest to describe, those in the middle, which define acceptable and unacceptable performance, are the most important. It is here, after all, that educators define their standards and specify the quality of work on which they insist and expect mastery. It is recommended that this level be described with particular care. And it is often best to start describing performance with the "proficient" level of performance, e.g., 3 points on a 4-point scale. When articulating this performance level, consider

– Content standards, specifically the concepts or skills students should understand or be able to use.
– Standards for Mathematical Practice, also described as habits of mind, mathematical process standards, etc. These reflect the kinds of behaviors proficient students engage in. The Common Core State Standards for Mathematics define eight of these standards, including the ability of students to model mathematically and look for and make use of the structure observed in a problem or their own work.
– Other affective skills demanded or required. For instance, are students required to collaborate as part of a group or team for this project?

Piloting the Rubric with Student Work

A rubric's purpose is in the evaluation of student work, and not until a rubric is used to evaluate actual student work will its authors know whether it is viable. Several steps are recommended.

Evaluating a Sample of Student Work

A good place to begin is to collect a small number of samples (about 8) of students' work, representing the full range of probable responses in the class. The sample should include those students from whom the best work would be expected, as well as those whose work might not be adequate. If possible, the pieces of work should be anonymous; they could be numbered and referred to by their numbers.

Then, with the rubric in hand, evaluate the student work using the draft rubric. The form shown in Table 7.2 may be used, with the criteria listed (or numbered) down the side, and the levels of performance for different students specified in the column corresponding to each one. Surveying the entire page then provides a summary of the levels of performance represented by the class as a whole, and can offer guidance as to the next instructional steps that may be needed.

Table 7.2 Performance Assessment Evaluation Results

Evaluator _____ Date _____

Task _____ Grade Level _____

Criteria	Student 1	Student 2	Student 3	Student 4

Inter-Rater Agreement

Even with careful design, it is possible that the rubric or the use of the rubric is not yet reliable. Unfortunately, educators often use education terminology with loosely defined meanings, such as rigor, understanding, etc. Or teachers, as colleagues, have dissonant expectations for student work. Addressing the potential lack of inter-rater agreement requires assistance from a colleague. It is recommended that another educator be introduced to the task and the rubric, and be provided with the same sample of student work initially used. This person should then evaluate the same students, and assign scores on each criterion based on the draft rubric.

Scores for each student on each criterion should then be compared. Clearly, the goal is for all scores to be the same, although this is unlikely to occur. Any discrepancies should then be discussed until the cause of the discrepancy is understood; most frequently, discrepancies are caused by a lack of clarity in the words used in the performance levels.

☑ **Professional Development Tip**

Setting Up Collaborative Sessions to Score Student Work

Teacher collaboration in the scoring of student work using a rubric (whether self-designed or part of a commercial program) offers a great opportunity for professional development. In addition to providing feedback to refine the design of the rubric, this activity provides teachers with an opportunity to

◆ Develop shared definitions of language and terminology.

◆ Bring differences in expectations for student performance to light and engage teachers in professional dialogue to address those differences.

◆ Share ideas on how to provide feedback to students.

◆ The experience also helps teachers understand the standards and learning progressions.

Collaborative scoring sessions can be set up among teachers at a grade level. Teachers can begin by selecting several pieces of work at each of the performance levels. Then they can give that work to colleagues to score and compare ratings along with their rationales. Alternatively, teachers can use the rubric along with a small set of student work samples and use a protocol to look carefully at 4 pieces of student work. Each teacher might bring work about which they have questions

(continued)

(continued)

or which doesn't fit neatly into one of the performance levels. The protocol could involve a descriptive review (in which low-inference evidence is collected) followed by an analysis of that evidence in which it is aligned to the criteria and performance levels of the rubric. The heart of the professional learning experience is the professional discourse that emerges as colleagues address ambiguity, uncertainty, disagreement, etc.

Revising the Rubric (and Possibly the Task)

As a result of evaluating student work and of comparing scores assigned with those of another educator, it is likely that the rubric (and possibly also the task) will require some revision. With luck, these revisions will not be extensive and will serve to clarify points of ambiguity.

Locating Anchor Papers

As a final step in rubric design, samples of student work that represent different points on the scale on each of the different criteria should be identified. By keeping these from year to year, it is possible to chart the course of general improvement of student work over time. In addition, only through the use of anchor papers can educators be sure that their standards are remaining the same, and are not subject to a gradual drift.

Involving Students in Rubric Design and Use

Many educators find that one of the most powerful uses of performance tasks and rubrics is to engage students actively in their design and use. That aspect of work with rubrics is described in this section, which may be used productively even with elementary students.

Advantages

Many advantages are cited for engaging students in the design of scoring rubrics. First and most important, by participating in the design of a scoring rubric, students are absolutely clear on the criteria by which their work will be evaluated. Furthermore, many teachers discover that students have good ideas to contribute to a rubric; they know, for example, the characteristics of an exemplary mathematics project.

But more importantly, when students know at the outset the criteria by which their work will be evaluated, and when they know the description of exemplary performance, they are better able (and more motivated) to produce high-quality work. The rubric provides guidance as to quality; students know exactly what they must do.

Consequently, many teachers find that when they involve students in the use of scoring rubrics, the quality of student work improves dramatically. So, when teachers have anchors (e.g., exemplary projects from a previous year) to illustrate good quality work to students, the general standard of work produced improves from year to year.

A Plan for Action

It is not obvious just how to engage students in designing and using scoring rubrics for evaluating student work. Some suggestions are offered here.

- ◆ *Starting with a draft.* A discussion with students about scoring rubrics should begin with a draft rubric already prepared by the teacher. The teacher should have some ideas, at least in general terms, of the criteria that should emerge from the discussion. Then, while students may suggest original ideas, the teacher can be sure that the final product includes all important aspects of performance. Another approach involves sharing the proficient criteria on the rubric for students. Students can they work to help define what additional criteria would be required for work to be considered exemplary. Similarly, they can help in defining the criteria for the lowest point on the scale. The distinction between the near-proficient and proficient levels of performance is often the hardest to make, and students would likely have the most difficulty defining it.

  Students may also be asked to contribute both to the generation of criteria and to the writing of performance descriptions. Many teachers are pleasantly surprised with the level of sophistication demonstrated by their students in this endeavor.

  The teacher should maintain control of the process of rubric design. While students will have excellent ideas, which should be accommodated to the maximum extent possible, the teacher should never relinquish control of the project to students.

- ◆ *Student self-assessment.* The first type of student use of a scoring rubric might be for students to evaluate their own work. Most teachers find that their students are, generally speaking, quite hard on themselves, in some cases more so than their teachers would be. Of course, clear performance descriptions will help in keeping evaluations consistent, but students frequently reveal a genuine concern for maintaining high standards, even when evaluating their own work. Task-specific rubrics that include expectations that reflect the demands of the performance task are less appropriate for students to use because they often include answers or strategies embedded as "look fors" in the rubric.

◆ *Peer assessment.* When the climate in a class is sufficiently supportive, students may be able to engage in peer assessment. Such an activity requires a high level of trust among students. However, if students have participated in the design of a scoring rubric, and have used it to evaluate their own work, they will generally be able to provide feedback to their peers in the same spirit of caring and support. When that occurs, the classroom becomes transformed into a true community of learners.

Adapting Existing Rubrics

Frequently, adapting an existing scoring rubric to one's own use may save much time and effort. Through this approach, educators can benefit from the work of others, and still have a rubric that reflects their own specific needs.

There are many sources of existing rubrics that may be adapted, in addition to those in this book. Many textbook publishers now offer some rubrics as part of their package. Some state departments of education and the National Council of Teachers of Mathematics (NCTM) have also created prototype rubrics. And with the widespread adoption of the Common Core State Standards, there are many tasks and accompanying rubrics available that are aligned to the standards used by teachers across the country.

Adapting the Criteria

When adapting rubrics, it is critical to ensure that the criteria apply to the task being assessed. Begin by asking

◆ What knowledge, skills, and understandings are required by the task?
◆ What dispositions, habits of mind, or practices do you expect students to demonstrate in performing the task? How will you measure them?
◆ What does the rubric offer to me as a user? How closely is it aligned with the objectives I have articulated for the task and my students?

One pitfall to be avoided is altering expectations of student work in response to a performance task to conform to a rubric. If the task encourages students to exhibit knowledge, skill, or understanding that are not reflected in the rubric, criteria related to these features should be added. Alternatively, if the rubric demands that students demonstrate knowledge, skill, or understanding unlikely to be exhibited in students' work, the criteria corresponding to those elements should be eliminated.

Adjusting the Performance Descriptions

Depending on the expectations and the particular task being assessed, the performance descriptions of a rubric may require adjustment. For example, using a rubric designed for a different grade or a previous set of standards may require adjustments in the descriptions of performance levels. Additionally, adoption of new standards may alter the definition of proficiency and, hence, the dividing line between acceptable and unacceptable performance.

Understanding an Adapted Rubric

When adapting a rubric, rather than developing it from scratch, it's important to be sure to work collaboratively to understand the expectations of the rubric. There are two key steps teachers can take to help ensure inter-rater agreement and consistent and fair use of a rubric, which are:

◆ Collaborate with colleagues to rewrite performance descriptions, where necessary. This can also be done with the goal of writing the descriptions in a student-friendly format. This has the added benefit of a version of the rubric that can clearly communicate your expectations with students. It also helps to clarify jargon, or overly vague language, as described earlier in this book.

◆ Apply the rubric to samples of student work from the task you intend to use it with.

When adopting or adapting a rubric, keep in mind that it should reflect your values and expectations. While good rubrics have the potential to change thinking about assessment, a thoughtfully designed task should not be compromised by a rubric designed for a different task or a different set of standards.

Piloting a Rubric with Students

Does the scoring rubric, as revised, still meet all the technical requirements described in Chapter 6? Do the descriptions of levels of performance use vivid words, and avoid comparative language? Are the distances between points on the scale approximately equal? Do the criteria reflect the most important aspects of performance?

Only an actual pilot of the revised task will elicit unambiguous answers to these questions. As educators and their students become more experienced in the use of performance tasks, however, this step may be combined with the first actual use of the task to evaluate student learning. That is, the task may be adapted as needed and used with students. Then, if it becomes apparent that the adaptation did not avoid all the pitfalls described above, the actual scores awarded to students can be adjusted accordingly. For example, if student performance is poor, but it becomes clear that the principal reason for the poor performance relates to lack of clarity in the directions, then the teacher's evaluation of student mastery must reflect that difficulty. Build stamina and perseverance in your daily teaching practices.

Chapter Summary

◆ Rubrics are complex instruments designed to evaluate complex performance. When designing or adapting rubrics, many factors must be considered. A critical step is the initial design of a rubric. For this process, a number of factors—such as whether it is generic or specific, the actual criteria, the number of points on the scale, and the language used to define the points—must be taken into account

◆ The number of points used to evaluate each criterion should, whenever possible, be an even number and contain enough points to meaningfully distinguish between levels of performance while not too many that it becomes time-consuming for teachers to use. Identifying the line between acceptable and unacceptable performance is a critical task when creating a rubric.

◆ Not until a scoring rubric has been piloted with actual student papers will its designers know whether it will prove to be effective. Collecting anchor papers that represent the actual work described in the rubric will ensure that the rubric can be applied fairly and reliably.

8

Early Elementary Mathematics Performance Tasks

This chapter has a collection of performance tasks and rubrics that are aligned with the mathematics standards, and that address all the important topics in primary school mathematics. They are arranged in alphabetical order (by title), with a table at the beginning of the chapter to assist you in locating tasks that you may want to use to assess specific skills and concepts. Some of the tasks include student work, which serves to illustrate the manner in which students interpret the directions given to them and to anchor the different points in the scoring rubrics.

You may find that the tasks are useful as presented. Alternatively, you may find that they can serve your purposes better if you adapt them. One way of adapting tasks is to incorporate names of people and places familiar to students in your class. This practice is frequently amusing to students, and therefore engaging.

In addition, tasks may be simplified or made more difficult by increasing or decreasing the amount of structure (or scaffolding) that students are provided. When you, the teacher, give guidance to students by outlining the steps needed in a solution, the resulting task is significantly easier (and less authentic). Similarly, when tasks are provided with considerable scaffolding, you can make them more complex by removing some or all of the scaffolding.

The rubrics presented in this book include criteria across three major dimensions of performance, namely a student's

- problem solving approach;
- accuracy, precision, and computational fluency; and
- ability to communicate his or her mathematical understandings, in pictures, words, and/or numbers.

These three criteria are designed to provide teachers with a comprehensive picture of students' conceptual understanding and procedural skill. "Problem solving approach" refers to students' ability to make sense of a problem, organize the components, select a strategy and implement it, or reason about how to solve the problem. "Accuracy, precision, and computational fluency" collectively refer to students' procedural fluency and ability to double-check to see if an answer is reasonable, possibly using another model or strategy. This dimension also includes key elements of precision identified in the Mathematical Practices, including labeling units and using precise mathematical language. Lastly, we assess students' "communication." Many of the performance tasks in this collection explicitly ask that students explain their thinking orally or in written form. In doing so, we ask them to engage in modeling mathematics, make use of structure and reason like a mathematician. Together, these three criteria define a mathematically proficient student. Beyond the skill and concept that a multiple-choice test can measure, tasks can assess proficiency with application, strategic thinking, and the practices that provide evidence of a deeper understanding.

Table 8.1 Early Elementary Tasks Alignment Chart

Task Name	Grade Level	Common Core Content Standards	Common Core Standards for Mathematical Practice
All in the Family	K-2	K.OA.A.1 Represent addition and subtraction with objects, fingers, mental images, drawings, sounds, acting out situations, verbal explanations, expressions, or equations. 1.OA.A.1 Use addition and subtraction within 20 to solve word problems involving situations of adding to, taking from, putting together, taking apart, and comparing, with unknowns in all positions. 2.OA.A.1 Use addition and subtraction within 100 to solve one-and two-step word problems involving situations of adding to, taking from, putting together, taking apart, and comparing, with unknowns in all positions.	SMP2 Reason abstractly and quantitatively. SMP8 Look for and express regularity in repeated reasoning.
Amazing Equations	K-2	K.OA.A.3 Decompose numbers less than or equal to 10 into pairs in more than one way, using objects or drawings, and record each decomposition by a drawing or equation. 1.OA.D.7 Understand the meaning of the equal sign, and determine if equations involving addition and subtraction are true or false. 1.OA.D.8 Determine the unknown whole number in an addition or subtraction equation relating to three whole numbers. 2.NBT.B.9 Explain why addition and subtraction strategies work, using place value and the properties of operations.	SMP1 Make sense of problems and persevere in solving them. SMP7 Look for and make use of structure.
Data Collecting	1-2	1.MD.C.4 Organize, represent, and interpret data with up to three categories; ask and answer questions about the total number of data points, how many in each category, and how many more or less are in one category than in another. 2.MD.D.10 Draw a picture graph and a bar graph to represent a data set with up to four categories. Solve simple put-together, take-apart, and compare problems using information presented in a bar graph.	SMP5 Use appropriate tools strategically. SMP8 Look for and express regularity in repeated reasoning.

(continued)

Table 8.1 *(continued)*

Task Name	Grade Level	Common Core Content Standards	Common Core Standards for Mathematical Practice
Detective Glyph	1-2	1.MD.C.4 Organize, represent, and interpret data with up to three categories; ask and answer questions about the total number of data points, how many in each category, and how many more or less are in one category than in another. 2.MD.D.10 Draw a picture graph and a bar graph to represent a data set with up to four categories. Solve simple put-together, take-apart, and compare problems using information presented in a bar graph.	SMP2 Reason abstractly and quantitatively. SMP4 Model with mathematics.
Extended Number Patterns	1-2	1.OA.A.1 Count to 120, starting at any number less than 120. In this range, read and write numerals and represent a number of objects with a written numeral. 1.NBT.C.4 Add within 100, including adding a two-digit number and a one-digit number, and adding a two-digit number and a multiple of 10, using concrete models or drawings and strategies based on place value, properties of operations, and / or the relationship between addition and subtraction; relate the strategy to a written method and explain the reasoning used. Understand that in adding two-digit numbers, one adds tens and tens, and ones and ones; and sometimes it is necessary to compose a ten.	SMP4 Model with mathematics. SMP7 Look for and make use of structure.
Fair Shares	K-2	K.CC.B.4 Understand the relationship between numbers and quantities; connect counting to cardinality. 1.OA.C.5 Relate counting to addition and subtraction (e.g., by counting on 2 to add 2). 2.OA.A.1 Use addition and subtraction within 100 to solve one- and two-step word problems involving situations of adding to, taking from, putting together, taking apart, and comparing, with unknowns in all positions, e.g., by using drawings and equations with a symbol for the unknown number to represent the problem.	SMP1 Make sense of problems and persevere in solving them. SMP5 Use appropriate tools strategically.

Fractions, Parts and Pieces	1-2	**1.G.A.2** Compose two-dimensional shapes (rectangles, squares, trapezoids, triangles, half-circles, and quarter-circles) or three-dimensional shapes (cubes, right rectangular prisms, right circular cones, and right circular cylinders) to create a composite shape, and compose new shapes from the composite shape. **1.G.A.3** Partition circles and rectangles into two and four equal shares; describe the shares using the words *halves, fourths,* and *quarters,* and use the phrases *half of, fourth of,* and *quarter of.* Describe the whole as two of, or four of the shares. Understand for these examples that decomposing into more equal shares creates smaller shares. **2.G.A.3** Partition circles and rectangles into two, three, or four equal shares; describe the shares using the words *halves, thirds, half of, a third of,* etc., and describe the whole as two halves, three thirds, four fourths. Recognize that equal shares or identical wholes need not have the same shape.	SMP1 Make sense of problems and persevere in solving them. SMP5 Use appropriate tools strategically.
Holiday Dinner	K-2	**K.OA.A.1** Represent addition and subtraction with objects, fingers, mental images, drawings, sounds, acting out situations, verbal explanations, expressions, or equations. **1.OA.A.1** Use addition and subtraction within 20 to solve word problems involving situations of adding to, taking from, putting together, taking apart, and comparing, with unknowns in all positions. **2.OA.A.1** Use addition and subtraction within 100 to solve one-and two-step word problems involving situations of adding to, taking from, putting together, taking apart, and comparing, with unknowns in all positions.	SMP2 Reason abstractly and quantitatively. SMP7 Look for and make use of structure.
How Many More?	K-2	**K.OA.A.3** Decompose numbers less than or equal to 10 into pairs in more than one way, e.g., by using objects or drawings, and record each decomposition by a drawing or equation. **1.OA.B.3** Apply properties of operations as strategies to add and subtract. Examples: If $8 + 3 = 11$ is known, then $3 + 8 = 11$ is also known. (Commutative property of addition.) To add $2 + 6 + 4$, the second two numbers can be added to make a ten, so $2 + 6 + 4 = 2 + 10 = 12$. (Associative property of addition.) *Students need not use formal terms for these properties.* **1.OA.B.4** Understand subtraction as an unknown-addend problem. For example, subtract $10 - 8$ by finding the number that makes 10 when added to 8.	SMP4 Model with mathematics. SMP6 Attend to precision.

(continued)

Table 8.1 (*continued*)

Task Name	Grade Level	Common Core Content Standards	Common Core Standards for Mathematical Practice
How Many More? (*continued*)		1.OA.C.6 Add and subtract within 20, demonstrating fluency for addition and subtraction within 10. Use strategies such as counting on; making ten (e.g., $8 + 6 = 8 + 2 + 4 = 10 + 4 = 14$); decomposing a number leading to a ten (e.g., $13 - 4 = 13 - 3 - 1 = 10 - 1 = 9$); using the relationship between addition and subtraction (e.g., knowing that $8 + 4 = 12$, one knows $12 - 8 = 4$); and creating equivalent but easier or known sums (e.g., adding $6 + 7$ by creating the known equivalent $6 + 6 + 1 = 12 + 1 = 13$). 2.OA.B.2 Fluently add and subtract within 20 using mental strategies. By end of Grade 2, know from memory all sums of two one-digit numbers.	
Is it 15?	K-1	K.G.B.5 Model shapes in the world by building shapes from components (e.g., sticks and clay balls) and drawing shapes. K.G.B.6 Compose simple shapes to form larger shapes. For example, "Can you join these two triangles with full sides touching to make a rectangle?" 1.G.A.2 Compose two-dimensional shapes (rectangles, squares, trapezoids, triangles, half-circles, and quarter-circles) or three-dimensional shapes (cubes, right rectangular prisms, right circular cones, and right circular cylinders) to create a composite shape, and compose new shapes from the composite shape.	SMP2 Reason abstractly and quantitatively. SMP5 Use appropriate tools strategically.
Losing Teeth	1-2	1.NBT.C.4 Add within 100, including adding a two-digit number and a one-digit number, and adding a two-digit number and a multiple of 10, using concrete models or drawings and strategies based on place value, properties of operations, and/or the relationship between addition and subtraction; relate the strategy to a written method and explain the reasoning used. Understand that in adding two-digit numbers, one adds tens and tens, ones and ones; and sometimes it is necessary to compose a ten. 2.NBT.B.5 Use place value understanding and properties of operations to add and subtract. Fluently add and subtract within 100 using strategies based on place value, properties of operations, and/or the relationship between addition and subtraction.	SMP1 Make sense of problems and persevere in solving them. SMP5 Use appropriate tools strategically.

Measure Me	K-2	K.MD.A.1 Describe measurable attributes of objects, such as length or weight. Describe several measurable attributes of a single object. 1.MD.A.1 Order three objects by length; compare the lengths of two objects indirectly by using a third object. 1.MD.A.2 Express the length of an object as a whole number of length units, by laying multiple copies of a shorter object (the length unit) end to end; understand that the length measurement of an object is the number of same-size length units that span it with no gaps or overlaps. *Limit to contexts where the object being measured is spanned by a whole number of length units with no gaps or overlaps.* 2.MD.A.1 Measure the length of an object by selecting and using appropriate tools such as rulers, yardsticks, meter sticks, and measuring tapes. 2.MD.A.2 Measure the length of an object twice, using length units of different lengths for the two measurements; describe how the two measurements relate to the size of the unit chosen. 2.MD.A.3 Estimate lengths using units of inches, feet, centimeters, and meters.	SMP 5 Use appropriate tools strategically. SMP6 Attend to precision.
Number Line	1-2	1.NBT.C.4 Use place value understanding and properties of operations to add and subtract. Add within 100, including adding a two-digit number and a one-digit number, and adding a two-digit number and a multiple of 10, using concrete models or drawings and strategies based on place value, properties of operations, and/or the relationship between addition and subtraction; relate the strategy to a written method and explain the reasoning used. Understand that in adding two-digit numbers, one adds tens and tens, ones and ones; and sometimes it is necessary to compose a ten. 1.NBT.C.5 Given a two-digit number, mentally find 10 more or 10 less than the number, without having to count; explain the reasoning used. 2.NBT.B.5 Fluently add and subtract within 100 using strategies based on place value, properties of operations, and/or the relationship between addition and subtraction. 2.NBT.B.7 Add and subtract within 1,000, using concrete models or drawings and strategies based on place value, properties of operations, and/or the relationship between addition and subtraction; relate the strategy to a written method. Understand that in adding or subtracting three-digit numbers, one adds or subtracts hundreds and hundreds, tens and tens, ones and ones; and sometimes it is necessary to compose or decompose tens or hundreds.	SMP6 Attend to precision. SMP 5 Use appropriate tools strategically.

(continued)

Table 8.1 (*continued*)

Task Name	Grade Level	Common Core Content Standards	Common Core Standards for Mathematical Practice
Number Trees	K-2	K.OA.A.3 Decompose numbers less than or equal to 10 into pairs in more than one way, e.g., by using objects or drawings, and record each decomposition by a drawing or equation (e.g., $5 = 2 + 3$ and $5 = 4 + 1$). K.OA.A.4 For any number from 1 to 9, find the number that makes 10 when added to the given number, e.g., by using objects or drawings, and record the answer with a drawing or equation. K.OA.A.5 Fluently add and subtract within 5. 1.OA.B.4 Understand subtraction as an unknown-addend problem. For example, subtract $10 - 8$ by finding the number that makes 10 when added to 8. 1.OA.C.6 Add and subtract within 20, demonstrating fluency for addition and subtraction within 10. Use strategies such as counting on; making ten (e.g., $8 + 6 = 8 + 2 + 4 = 10 + 4 = 14$); decomposing a number leading to a ten (e.g., $13 - 4 = 13 - 3 - 1 = 10 - 1 = 9$); using the relationship between addition and subtraction (e.g., knowing that $8 + 4 = 12$, one knows $12 - 8 = 4$); and creating equivalent but easier or known sums (e.g., adding $6 + 7$ by creating the known equivalent $6 + 6 + 1 = 12 + 1 = 13$). 2.OA.A.1 Use addition and subtraction within 100 to solve one- and two-step word problems involving situations of adding to, taking from, putting together, taking apart, and comparing, with unknowns in all positions, e.g., by using drawings and equations with a symbol for the unknown number to represent the problem. 2.OA.A.2 Fluently add and subtract within 20 using mental strategies. By end of Grade 2, know from memory all sums of two one-digit numbers.	SMP2 Reason abstractly and quantitatively. SMP8 Look for and express regularity in repeated reasoning.
Paper Quilts	K-2	K.G.B.5 Model shapes in the world by building shapes from components (e.g., sticks and clay balls) and drawing shapes. K.G.B.6 Compose simple shapes to form larger shapes. For example, "Can you join these two triangles with full sides touching to make a rectangle?"	SMP4 Model with mathematics. SMP7 Look for and make use of structure.

		1.G.A.2 Compose two-dimensional shapes (rectangles, squares, trapezoids, triangles, half-circles, and quarter-circles) or three-dimensional shapes (cubes, right rectangular prisms, right circular cones, and right circular cylinders) to create a composite shape, and compose new shapes from the composite shape.	
Pizza Night	1-2	2.G.A.3 Partition circles and rectangles into two, three, or four equal shares, describe the shares using the words *halves, thirds, half of, a third of*, etc., and describe the whole as two halves, three thirds, four fourths. Recognize that equal shares of identical wholes need not have the same shape.	
		1.OA.A.1 Use addition and subtraction within 20 to solve word problems involving situations of adding to, taking from, putting together, taking apart, and comparing, with unknowns in all positions, e.g., by using objects, drawings, and equations with a symbol for the unknown number to represent the problem.	SMP3 Construct viable arguments and critique the reasoning of others.
		2.OA.A.1 Use addition and subtraction within 100 to solve one- and two-step word problems involving situations of adding to, taking from, putting together, taking apart, and comparing, with unknowns in all positions, e.g., by using drawings and equations with a symbol for the unknown number to represent the problem.	SMP4 Model with mathematics.
The Same Size as Me	K-2	K.MD.A.1 Describe measurable attributes of objects, such as length or weight. Describe several measurable attributes of a single object.	SMP1 Make sense of problems and persevere in solving them.
		1.MD.A.1 Order three objects by length; compare the lengths of two objects indirectly by using a third object.	SMP5 Use appropriate tools strategically.
		1.MD.A.2 Express the length of an object as a whole number of length units, by laying multiple copies of a shorter object (the length unit) end to end; understand that the length measurement of an object is the number of same-size length units that span it with no gaps or overlaps.	
		2.MD.A.1 Measure the length of an object by selecting and using appropriate tools such as rulers, yardsticks, meter sticks, and measuring tapes.	
		2.MD.A.2 Measure the length of an object twice, using length units of different lengths for the two measurements; describe how the two measurements relate to the size of the unit chosen.	
		2.MD.A.3 Estimate lengths using units of inches, feet, centimeters, and meters.	

(continued)

Table 8.1 *(continued)*

Task Name	Grade Level	Common Core Content Standards	Common Core Standards for Mathematical Practice
Shapes in My World	K-2	K.G.A.1 Describe objects in the environment using names of shapes, and describe the relative positions of these objects using terms such as above, below, beside, in front of, behind, and next to. K.G.A.2 Correctly name shapes regardless of their orientations or overall size. 1.G.A.1 Distinguish between defining attributes (e.g., triangles are closed and three-sided) versus non-defining attributes (e.g, color, orientation, overall size); build and draw shapes to possess defining attributes. 2.G.A.1 Recognize and draw shapes having specified attributes, such as a given number of angles or a given number of equal faces. Identify triangles, quadrilaterals, pentagons, hexagons, and cubes.	SMP4 Model with mathematics. SMP7 Look for and make use of structure.
Story Problems	K-2	K.OA.A.1 Understand addition as putting together and adding to, and understanding subtraction as taking apart and taking from. Represent addition and subtraction with objects, fingers, mental images, drawings, sounds (e.g., claps), acting out situations, verbal explanations, expressions, or equations. K.OA.A.2 Solve addition and subtraction word problems, and add and subtract within 10, e.g., by using objects or drawings to represent the problem. 1.OA.A.1 Use addition and subtraction within 20 to solve word problems involving situations of adding to, taking from, putting together, taking apart, and comparing, with unknowns in all positions, e.g., by using objects, drawings, and equations with a symbol for the unknown number to represent the problem. 1.OA.A.2 Solve word problems that call for addition of three whole numbers whose sum is less than or equal to 20, e.g., by using objects, drawings, and equations with a symbol for the unknown number to represent the problem.	SMP1 Make sense of problems and persevere in solving them. SMP8 Look for and express regularity in repeated reasoning.

		2.NBT.B.5 Fluently add and subtract within 100 using strategies based on place value, properties of operations, and/or the relationship between addition and subtraction. 2.NBT.B.7 Add and subtract within 1,000, using concrete models or drawings and strategies based on place value, properties of operations, and/or the relationship between addition and subtraction; relate the strategy to a written method. Understand that in adding or subtracting three-digit numbers, one adds or subtracts hundreds and hundreds, tens and tens, ones and ones; and sometimes it is necessary to compose or decompose tens or hundreds.	
Word Problem Types	K-2	K.OA.A.1 Understand addition as putting together and adding to, and understanding subtraction as taking apart and taking from. Represent addition and subtraction with objects, fingers, mental images, drawings, sounds (e.g., claps), acting out situations, verbal explanations, expressions, or equations. 1.OA.A.1 Use addition and subtraction within 20 to solve word problems involving situations of adding to, taking from, putting together, taking apart, and comparing, with unknowns in all positions, e.g., by using objects, drawings, and equations with a symbol for the unknown number to represent the problem. 1.OA.A.2 Solve word problems that call for addition of three whole numbers whose sum is less than or equal to 20, e.g., by using objects, drawings, and equations with a symbol for the unknown number to represent the problem. 2.OA.A.1 Use addition and subtraction within 100 to solve one- and two-step word problems involving situations of adding to, taking from, putting together, taking apart, and comparing, with unknowns in all positions, e.g., by using drawings and equations with a symbol for the unknown number to represent the problem.	SMP1 Make sense of problems and persevere in solving them. SMP8 Look for and express regularity in repeated reasoning.

ALL IN MY FAMILY

Mathematics Assessed

- ◆ Counting and Cardinality
- ◆ Operations and Algebraic Thinking
- ◆ Number Operations and Base Ten
- ◆ Habits of Mind
- ◆ Reasoning and Explaining.

Directions to the Student

- ◆ Draw a picture of the people that live with you.
- ◆ How many people in your family? Include yourself _____
- ◆ How many eyes in your family? _____
- ◆ How many fingers in your family? _____
- ◆ What else would you like to count? _____
- ◆ How many _____ in your family?
- ◆ What patterns did you notice?

Students are asked to illustrate their thinking, write an equation and a few sentences to show and tell about their work.

About This Task

This task requires students to apply number counting patterns, by 2s, 5s, and 10s. Younger students may still need to use a one-to-one correspondence. Their illustrations give us insight to the process they have applied. Written equations and sentences support their thinking.

Solution

Solutions vary according to the number of people in the student's family. Students are asked to provide an illustration, equation, and an idea of their own. Students may choose noses, toes, eyebrows, and so forth. More experienced students may notice patterns and relationships between hands and feet, ears and eyes, noses and mouths, and so forth.

Rubric

	Level One	Level Two	Level Three	Level Four
Problem Solving Approach	The information isn't represented or is unorganized.	Most of the information is represented.	All the information is represented.	The information is well-planned, organized, and complete.
Accuracy and Precision	The computation and writing are inaccurate.	The computation and writing contain minor errors.	The computation and writing are accurate and complete.	The computation and writing are above grade-level standards.
Communication	The conclusions are incomplete and invalid.	The conclusions reveal a partial understanding of counting patterns and notation.	The conclusions show an understanding of counting patterns and notation.	The conclusions show an advanced application of counting patterns and notation.

Samples of Student Work

Level One

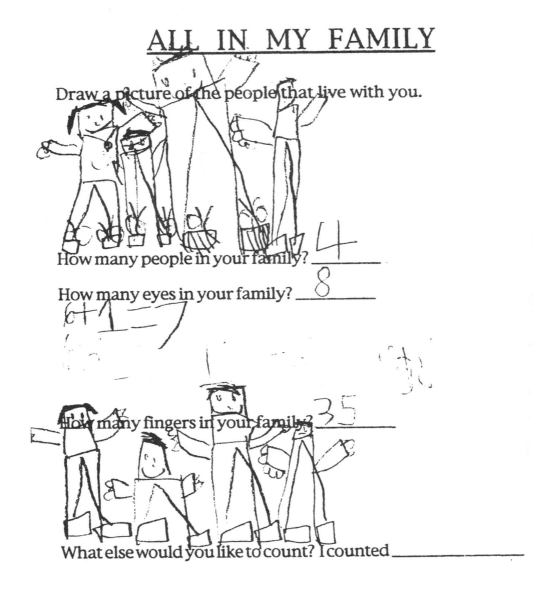

ALL IN MY FAMILY

Draw a picture of the people that live with you.

How many people in your family? 4

How many eyes in your family? 8

6 + 1 = 7

How many fingers in your family? 35

What else would you like to count? I counted _____

This response represents four family members. It does not represent the number of eyes. The equation $6 + 1 = 7$ is not relevant. Only some of the fingers in the family were illustrated and counted. No additional idea was developed.

Level Two

Draw a picture of the people that live with you.

How many people in your family? _____

How many eyes in your family? _16_

How many fingers in your family? _70_

What else would you like to count? I counted three are
16 eyes in my Family
there are 8 Noses in my
Family
16+8=23

This response represents eight family members, their eyes, and fingers. Minor errors are found in the computation of fingers and the equation 16 + 8 = 23. One-by-one counting of noses communicates a partial understanding of counting patterns.

Level Three

Draw a picture of the people that live with you.

How many people in your family? 4

How many eyes in your family? 8

$| + | + | + | + | + | + | + | - | = 8$

How many fingers in your family? 40

$| + | + | + | + | + | + | + | + | + | + |$
$| + | + | + | + | + | + | + | + | + | + |$
$| + | + | + | + | + | + | + | + | = 40$

What else would you like to count? I counted _____

I love my mom and Dad.

This response was difficult to evaluate. The work completed was accurate, but the student failed to answer the last question. The "I love my mom and dad" statement is typical of primary students who are so personally involved in their work, that they write comments that are not necessarily mathematical. During the oral presentation, the student was able to quickly self-correct, count the heads in the family, and report that there were four. The written equation demonstrates one-by-one counting.

Level Three

Draw a picture of the people that live with you.

How many people in your family? 6

How many eyes in your family? 12

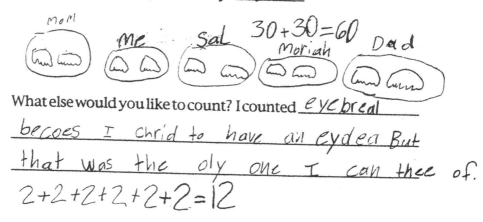

How many fingers in your family? 60

What else would you like to count? I counted _eyebreal_

becoes I chrid to have an eydea But
that was the oly one I can thee of.

$2+2+2+2+2+2=12$

This response is a solid Level Three. The elements are represented; equations and sentences are accurate; and the presentation showed a basic understanding of counting patterns. (Jessica's fingers were not drawn but were counted.) The student writes, *"I counted eyebrows because I tried to have an idea but that was the only one I can think of."*

Level Four

Draw a picture of the people that live with you.

Draw a picture of the people that live with you.

How many people in your family? _____5_____.

How many eyes in your family? ___10___.

$4 + 6 = 10$ $5 + 5 = 10$ $1+1+1+|+|+|+|+|+|+1 = 10$

How many fingers in your family? ___50___

I cated my familys fingers.

$10 + 10 + 10 + 10 + 10 = 50$

What else would you like to count? I counted How many fingers and how many eyes alltogather there are 60

$50 + 10 = 60$

This response is well planned, detailed, and mathematically accurate. Notice the one-by-one counting and as well as the counting by 10s. The explanation revealed the student's understanding that counting by 1s would not be efficient with so many fingers; therefore, counting by 10s was applied.

AMAZING EQUATIONS

Mathematics Assessed

- ◆ Counting and Cardinality
- ◆ Operations and Algebraic Thinking
- ◆ Number Operations and Base Ten
- ◆ Habits of Mind
- ◆ Seeing Structure and Generalizing.

Directions to the Student

- ◆ Choose a number between 1 and 20 (for kindergarten, 11–120 for first grade, and between 120 and 1,000 for second grade).
- ◆ Record your number at the top of your paper.
- ◆ Write at least 10 equivalent equations for that number. You may draw pictures to illustrate your thinking. The equations can be written horizontally or vertically.
- ◆ Share your equations with a partner.

About This Task

You will want to model this activity for the whole group first. This task requires students to communicate their understanding of a numerical quantity and notation in written form. This activity can be used in math journals, from time to time, to show student progress through the school year.

Solution

Solutions will vary. Assessment of student work is based on the quantity, quality, and accuracy of the equivalent equations. Expect at least 5 equations for kindergarten at the beginning of the year, working up to 10 equations. In first and second grade, expect to see an understanding of place value (ones, tens, and hundreds) reflected in the equations. Encourage more capable students to work at a more challenging level with addition, subtraction, multiplication, and division, or multi-step equations.

Rubric

	Level One	Level Two	Level Three	Level Four
Problem Solving Approach	The information is random; the display is difficult to follow.	The information is organized; the equation display is easy to follow.	The information, including the required number of equations, are displayed in a systematic way.	The information includes evidence of planning; it might include vertical and horizontal equations, and/or equivalent expressions like $7 + 8 = 9 + 6$.
Accuracy and Precision	The equations are incomplete or inaccurate.	The equations are mostly complete and accurate.	The equations are complete and accurate.	The equations reflect an understanding of properties and inverse operations.
Communication	Explanation is unclear; shows little understanding of the concept.	Explanation has minor errors; applied some numeric understanding.	Explanation is clear and communicates numeric understanding.	Explanation is well-presented; contains evidence of advanced mathematical reasoning.

Samples of Student Work

Level Three

$27-1=26$
$28-2=26$
$25+1=26$
$26+0=26$
$1+55=26$
$27-1=26$
$33-6=26$
$6+20=26$
$20+6=26$
$19+7=26$
$7+19=26$
$13+10+6=26$
$9+9\ 5=26$
$5+5\ 15+5+6=26$
$6+6\ 8+6=26$

$1+$ $1+$ $1+$ $1+$ $1+$ $1+$ $1+$ $1+$
$1+$ $1+$ $1+$ $1+$ $1+$ $1+$ $1+$
$1+$ $1+$ $1+$ $1+$ $1+$ $1+$ $1+$
$1+$ $1+$ $1+$ $1+$ $1=26$
☺$+26$
$17+8=26$

Only a Level Three response is shown. This is a first grade sample. The student generated many more examples than required. All but three are accurate. Notice the patterns in $6 + 20 = 26$, $20 + 6 = 26$. This student is applying the communicative property of addition. The happy face before + 26 is really a zero!

DATA COLLECTING

Mathematics Assessed

- ◆ Counting and Cardinality
- ◆ Measurement and Data
- ◆ Reasoning and Explaining
- ◆ Modeling and Using Tools.

Directions to the Student

Today, you'll each have a chance to ask a question and collect data about something you are interested in learning about each other. You will graph your data using a bar graph and present your information in writing and orally to the class.

We will graph our data using a bar graph and present our information in writing and orally to the class.

Choose a question, for example, "_____". Ask the question of each person in our room and decide how you will keep track of the answers. There are ___ students and ___ adults in our room today. (Record the total on the board.)

There are different methods of keeping track of the information, for example a yes/no list or a Venn Diagram.

Ask each person your question and keep track of the answers using your plan. Then create a bar graph showing your results. Remember to label your columns, rows, and to title your graph. When you have completed your graph, write two "I learned" statements about your data.

Oral Presentation: Tell us what your question was and how you collected the information. Show us your graph and tell us what you learned. Ask your classmates to share any questions or comments they may have.

About This Task

This task requires students to collect, graph, and communicate information through a graphic, written, and oral presentation. They must choose an appropriate question and an effective method for collecting their data. Directions could be read out loud and posted for students to review.

The teacher can assess each child's work when the students are sharing it with their classmates.

Solution

Solutions will vary depending on the types of questions, the methods for collecting the data, and the writing ability of the individual students. This is an excellent task for comparing strategies and graphic organization.

Rubric

	Level One	Level Two	Level Three	Level Four
Problem Solving Approach	Information is misrepresented or incomplete.	Information is mostly complete; approach is not organized.	Information is complete; approach is workable.	Information is complete; approach consists of a highly efficient collection strategy.
Accuracy and Precision	The bar graph display is not labeled, or inaccurate and incomplete.	The bar graph display is incomplete or the representation is in a non-standard format.	The bar graph display has two of three labeled (title, columns, rows) correctly; data is complete.	The bar graph display is neat, accurate, labeled, and shows evidence of planning.
Communication (Written Statement)	No statement is provided, or it is unrelated or unclear.	One statement shows some understanding of process.	Two statements summarize the information.	At least two statements are included and analyze the data beyond the obvious.
Communication (Oral Presentation)	The presentation is missing or not on topic.	The presentation has errors in the sequence; or incomplete thoughts.	The presentation is complete and accurate.	The presentation shows mastery of the research process.

Samples of Student Work

Level One

What is your favorite ice-cream?

cat/t vanla cat/l
cat/t v.Nci
cat/t vana.Jca
roak cock vhia
cat/t vna
cook/y oow vanla
boal aun cat/t
boal aun cat/00
cooky Doow

Choco										
Vanilla										
Bubble Gum										
Cookie Dough										
Rocky Road										

I learned that more kids like Vanilla.

This response shows a random collection of information. With some teacher intervention, the student was able to graph the information. However, there are 19 answers on the collection page, and 21 on the graph. There is no title, and columns are not numbered. The written statement is accurate but limited in mathematical communication.

Level Two

Hardly any body likes purple.

This student used the initials of the students she surveyed so that she could remember whom she had already polled. There is no systematic recording other than that the color matches the response. The graph is accurate, but missing a title and numbered columns. The written statement shows some understanding of the information collected.

Level Three

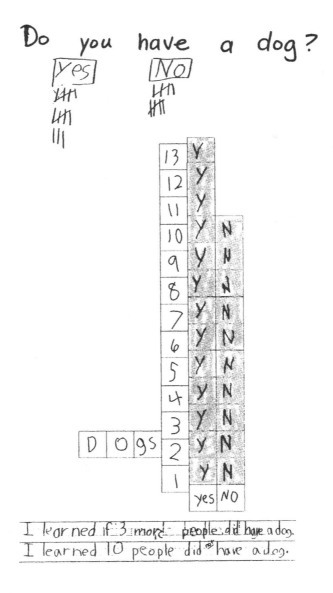

I learned if 3 more people did have a dog.
I learned 10 people did have a dog.

This response is a complete and organized collection of information. The bar graph is labeled with a title, columns and rows. The written statements reflect errors in thought that were clarified and self-corrected during the oral presentation. The student meant to say: "I learned that if three or more people did have a dog, *it would be tied.*" Primary students don't always proof their written work. The oral explanations allow students a forum for editing their work.

Level Four

have you had spider bites
before?

yes

‖‖ ‖‖ ‖

No

‖‖ ‖‖ ‖

11				
10			S	b
9			p	i
8			i	t
7			d	e
6			e	s
5			r	
4				
3				
2				
1				
	yes	no		

I learned it was half and half
11 kids did not have a spider
bites and 11 kids did have
1 spider bites.

I learned there's a lot of
people that have spider
in their house because
there was a lot of people
that had spider bites.

This response is complete, accurate, and neat. The student made a pattern when she colored in the "no" responses and drew black spiders for the "yes" responses. The written statements demonstrate an understanding of fractions (*half and half*) and an analysis of where spiders come from *"in their house."*

DETECTIVE GLYPH

Mathematics Assessed

- ◆ Operations and Algebraic Thinking
- ◆ Measurement and Data
- ◆ Reasoning and Explaining
- ◆ Modeling and Using Tools.

Directions to the Student

In ancient times, stories were told with pictures. These pictures, sometimes found on cave walls, were called hieroglyphics. Together we're going to create a legend, using different attributes, which tells us something special about each of you. I will make a chart of the attributes we chose for us to follow when we create our art project. The project you will create is called a glyph.

When you have finished making your art project, write out three clues using the legend to help your classmates figure out who you are.

About This Task

In this task, students are asked to represent, analyze, and interpret information from a legend or key. Although many ready-made idea books are available on the market, students may enjoy making up their own legends. Students will enjoy the challenge of being detectives, especially with a class across the hall. It will also discourage just remembering "who did what" during the activity.

This activity can also be used to sort, diagram, and graph group characteristics; for instance, boys who have brown eyes or girls who are seven.

Solution

Solutions will vary according to the legend and seasonal thematic project you create with your students. Some attributes that can be included are: boy–girl, birthday, age, hobby, favorite food, favorite color, type of shoe, family members, ride-walk-bus to school, and eye color.

Rubric

	Level One	Level Two	Level Three	Level Four
Problem Solving Approach	The model does not correspond to the legend.	The model mostly corresponds to the legend.	The model corresponds to the legend.	The model corresponds to the legend; includes additional details.
Accuracy and Precision	Inaccurate interpretation of the attributes.	Mostly accurate interpretation of the attributes.	Accurate interpretation of attributes.	Accurate interpretation of attributes leads student to abstract conclusions.
Communication	Response has fewer than two clues; unclear response.	Response has fewer than three clues; response is incomplete.	Response has three complete clues.	Response has complete clues and demonstrates a synthesis of the clues/attributes.

On the next page is an example of a chart which lists the attributes of the glyphs. The attributes are selected by the students and the teacher together. Below the chart is an example of a student's drawing of a ladybird (or ladybug). The drawing indicates that the student does not like ladybirds (no circles at the end of the antennae); the student has never seen a ladybird (2 inch legs); and the student has been bitten by a bug (three dots).

Do you like ladybirds?

Yes \ /   No \ /

Have you ever caught a ladybird?

Yes *3" legs*   No *2" legs*

Have you been bitten by a bug?

Yes *3 dots*   No *2 dots*

Have you seen a _____ ladybird?

Red   Gray

Black   Yellow-green

EXTENDED NUMBER PATTERNS

Mathematics Assessed

- ◆ Operations and Algebraic Thinking
- ◆ Number Operations and Base Ten
- ◆ Modeling and Using Tools
- ◆ Seeing Structure and Generalizing.

Directions to the Student

- ◆ Choose an object to count (for example, stickers or stamps).
- ◆ Notice something about this object that you can count by 2s, 5s, 10s, or any other number.
- ◆ Number your construction paper on the left side from 1 to 6.
- ◆ Arrange your objects on your paper with 1 object in the first row, 2 objects in the second row, and so on.
- ◆ Write an equation to show how you counted the number of items (2s, 5s, 10s).

First and second grade students might be asked to complete a 100 or 120 chart, to show the counting pattern. They can also be asked to write the corresponding repeated addition or multiplication equations.

About This Task

This task can apply to a wide range of student abilities. Younger students should have multiple whole-group experiences with real objects before they move to an abstract paper model. Whole-group practice will scaffold your students' ability to follow with independent work. This is a visual preparation for the multiplication model through repeated addition and skip counting.

An oral presentation to the class or brief conference with a teacher allows the students to share their understandings.

Solution

The students will need to complete the correct counting pattern for 2, 5, or 10. Children who are capable of more challenging work should be encouraged to work with other number patterns.

Rubric

	Level One	Level Two	Level Three	Level Four
Problem Solving Approach	The chart is unorganized; incomplete.	The chart is mostly organized; not in the format suggested and information is incomplete.	The chart is organized and includes numbered rows; observation statements and equations.	The chart is well organized and complete.
Accuracy and Precision	The chart and statements have major computation errors.	The chart and statements have mostly accurate computation.	The chart, equations, and statements reflect accurate computation.	The chart, equations, and statements reflect advanced computation strategies and operations.
Communication	The explanation is unclear.	The explanation shows an incomplete understanding of counting patterns.	The explanation includes the visual model, equations and mathematical language.	The explanation is clear with new generalizations about counting patterns, operations and/or properties.

Samples of Student Work

Level Three

Star Extended Number Pattern

1 star has 5 points. 5+0=5

2 stars have 10 points. 5+5=10

3 stars have 15 points. 5+5+5=15

4 stars have 20 points. 5+5+5+5=20

5 stars have 25 points. 5+5+5+5+5=25

6 stars have 30 points. 5+5+5+5+5+5=30

7 stars have 35 points. 5+5+5+5+5+5+5=35

8 stars have 40 points. 5+5+5+5+5+5+5+5=40

1	2	3	4	5	6	7	8	9	10
11	12	13	14	15	16	17	18	19	20
21	22	23	24	25	26	27	28	29	30
31	32	33	34	35	36	37	38	39	40
41	42	43	44	45	46	47	48	49	50
51	52	53	54	55	56	57	58	59	60
61	62	63	64	65	66	67	68	69	70
71	72	73	74	75	76	77	78	79	80
81	82	83	84	85	86	87	88	89	90
91	92	93	94	95	96	97	98	99	100

Only a Level Three is shown. This response is an example of a Level Three: a complete and accurate visual model of number counting patterns. Note the inclusion of the 100 matrix as additional support for the sentences and equations.

FAIR SHARES

Mathematics Assessed

- ◆ Counting and Cardinality
- ◆ Operations and Algebraic Thinking
- ◆ Number Operations and Base Ten
- ◆ Geometry
- ◆ Habits of Mind
- ◆ Modeling and Using Tools.

Directions to the Student

- ◆ Your teacher has brought a bag of candy to share with the class. Imagine these red tile are candy pieces. There are _____ pieces of candy all together.
- ◆ How many children are in your class? _____
- ◆ How many pieces of candy will YOU get if everyone gets a fair share? _____
- ◆ Show your thinking. Draw, write an equation, and write a few sentences that tell about your thinking.

About This Task

In this task, students are asked to identify the important elements of the problem and to illustrate their own model for division. Primary students have not yet been introduced to formal strategies, including algorithms, for division. Their approach will reflect their number sense, conceptual understanding, and application of divisions with a likely remainder. This task was created with candy, but could be duplicated with healthier choices like apples.

Solution

Solutions will vary depending on your class size and the number of pieces of candy. This task can be easily modified for kindergarten students by reducing the number of pieces of candy in the bag, to double the number of students. First graders might enjoy the challenge of considering what to do with a remainder.

Rubric

	Level One	Level Two	Level Three	Level Four
Problem Solving Approach	The information is disorganized or incomplete.	The information is mostly complete; no visible solution.	The drawing shows the information in the problem.	The drawing shows a complete representation of the information and solution.
Accuracy and Precision	The equations and sentences have major errors.	The equations and sentences have minor errors.	The equations and sentences are accurate.	The equation and sentences show an advanced understanding of division/ fractions.
Communication	The explanation shows a mis-understanding of fair shares.	The explanation shows a partial understanding of division as fair shares.	The explanation shows a reasonable solution to the problem.	The explanation reflects a complete rationale for the division process, equal shares, and/or fractions.

Samples of Student Work

Level One

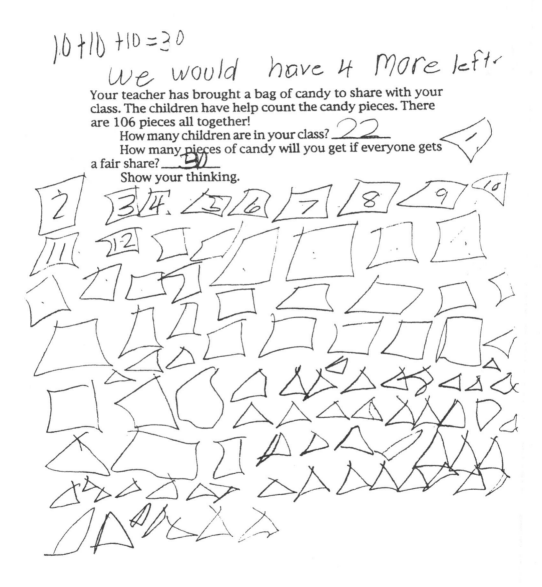

$10 + 10 + 10 = 30$

We would have 4 More left·

Your teacher has brought a bag of candy to share with your class. The children have help count the candy pieces. There are 106 pieces all together!

How many children are in your class? __22__

How many pieces of candy will you get if everyone gets a fair share? __30__

Show your thinking.

This response is difficult to understand, random, and incomplete. The student began drawing 106 pieces of candy, tried numbering them, and wrote an equation that is accurate but not relevant to the problem.

Level Two

FAIR SHARES

Your teacher has brought a bag of candy to share with your class. The children have help count the candy pieces. There are 106 pieces all together!

How many children are in your class? _____

How many pieces of candy will you get if everyone gets a fair share? _4_____

Show your thinking.

$$5 + 5 + 5 + 5 + 5 + 5 + 5 + 5 + 5 + 5 + 5 + 5$$
$$+5 + 5 + 5 + 5 + 5 + 5 + 5 + 5 + 5 + 5 + 5$$

This response has a drawing of 22 children and the pieces of candy that were passed out, one by one. The student didn't deal with the remainder and the equation on the back didn't match the solution.

Level Three

Your teacher has brought a bag of candy to share with your class. The children have help count the candy pieces. There are 106 pieces all together!

How many children are in your class? __22__

How many pieces of candy will you get if everyone gets a fair share? __5__

Show your thinking.

their is 0 lift

One of the people got 1 but he only wont one.

This response shows the student's thinking, 22 student faces, and counting by 5s. When the student realized he would be over the amount, he solved the problem by giving the last child only 1. He further justified his answer by stating he only wanted one.

Level Three

Your teacher has brought a bag of candy to share with your class. The children have help count the candy pieces. There are 106 pieces all together!

How many children are in your class? __22__

How many pieces of candy will you get if everyone gets a fair share? __4__

Show your thinking.

4+4+4+4 +4 +4 +4+4 +4 +4 +4 +4 = 90
+4 + 4 +4 +4 +4 +4+4
4+4+4+4+ 4 = 90 4 +4 +4 +4+4+4+4

I drew 22 X's.

I gave each X a piece. And anoter and another. anoter gntell I was done. I had 17 left over.

X X X X X X X Y Y X X X X X X X X X X X X X

This student drew 22 Xs to represent the children in the class. He gave each X an apple, then another, and another until he was done. The equation doesn't equal 90 and the remainder is not 17. The student self-corrected during his explanation. Students will often need this presentation time to rethink their solutions and adjust their errors.

Level Four

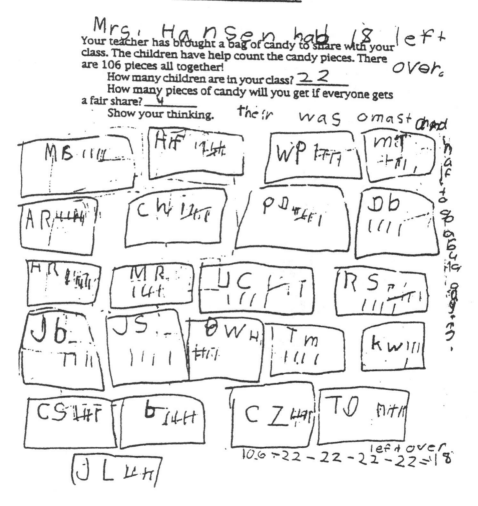

FAIR SHARES

Your teacher has brought a bag of candy to share with your class. The children have help count the candy pieces. There are 106 pieces all together!

How many children are in your class? __22__

How many pieces of candy will you get if everyone gets a fair share? __4__

Show your thinking.

This response shows evidence of planning. The student used boxes, student initials, and tally marks. The equation at the top reflects addition and the one at the bottom reflects subtraction accurately. The student gave the teacher the large remainder, and also noticed, "There was almost enough to go around again."

FRACTIONS, PARTS, AND PIECES

Mathematics Assessed

◆ Geometry
◆ Habits of Mind
◆ Modeling and Using Tools.

Directions to the Students

Part 1: Divide each square into four equal pieces, in a different way (fourths).

Part 2: Kale ate 2 halves of his brownie for snack. His sister Kait ate 4 fourths of her brownie. Kait said she ate more of her brownie.

Is she correct?   YES   NO

Use pictures, numbers and words to show your thinking.

About This Task

In this task, students are asked to divide a rectangle (square) into four equal parts, in three different ways. Students will describe the shares using precise math language, equal parts, halves, fourths and compare 2 halves and 4 fourths. The big idea in this task is to recognize that equal shares of the same whole, are not always the same shape.

Solution

Students generally divide the region in half, and then half again, creating either 4 squares or 4 thin rectangles (vertical or horizontal. Some students will also create a third example, using 2 diagonal lines, making 4 triangles. Understanding that these triangles have the same area, but don't look at all like a square or rectangle, is a cognitive shift in geometric thinking and fraction discovering.

Rubric

	Level One	Level Two	Level Three	Level Four
Problem Solving Approach	Information is random or missing.	Information is present but difficult to follow.	Information is organized; drawing and notation is complete.	Information is planned and presented in an efficient way.
Accuracy and Precision	1 example correctly reflects 4 equal parts.	2 examples correctly reflect 4 equal parts.	3 examples correctly reflect 4 equal parts.	Correctly connects the 4 equal parts with an understanding of the same space/area, or that the shapes can change depending on how you partition the square.
Communication	Explanation shows no understanding of halves and fourths.	Explanation shows an understanding of halves and fourths; not equivalence (2/2 = 4/4).	Explanation shows an understanding of equivalence with pictures, numbers or words.	Explanation shows an understanding of fraction concepts; using precise mathematical vocabulary.

HOLIDAY DINNER

Mathematics Assessed

- ◆ Counting and Cardinality
- ◆ Operations and Algebraic Thinking
- ◆ Number Operations and Base Ten
- ◆ Reasoning and Explaining
- ◆ Seeing Structure and Generalizing.

Directions to the Student

Your extended family is coming to your house for the holidays. It's your job to set the table with a knife, fork, and spoon at each place setting. How many pieces of silverware will you need to set the table? Show and tell how you know.

I have _____ people coming to dinner.
I will need _____ pieces of silverware.
I know because _____
My equation is _____

About This Task

This task requires students to know how many people are in their extended family. They need to draw a model for an abstract concept (counting by three) without formal multiplication instruction. Some children will solve the problem with one-by-one counting; others may apply a counting pattern of three. Encourage young children to illustrate each member of their family and to use cubes or some other available manipulative to solve the task more concretely.

Solution

Solutions will vary depending on the size of the extended family. Students enjoy doing this task around the seasonal holidays. Many of them actually have this chore in their home. Complete responses will include an illustration, an equation, and a sentence about the student's thinking.

Rubric

	Level One	Level Two	Level Three	Level Four
Problem Solving Approach	Information is random or incomplete.	Information is mostly complete and organized.	Information is complete and organized.	Information is presented with an efficient strategy.
Accuracy and Precision	The solution is inaccurate; illustration, equation, and/or sentence.	The solution is mostly accurate; illustration, equation, and/or sentence.	The solution is accurate and includes an illustration, equation, and sentence.	The solution is accurate and complete. Student demonstrates efficient counting strategies.
Communication	The explanation is minimal, with invalid conclusions.	The explanation is difficult to interpret or work towards a final conclusion.	The explanation supports a valid conclusions and understanding.	The explanation includes a conclusion that demonstrates a synthesis of task.

Samples of Student Work

Level One

Your extended family is coming to your house for the holidays. It's your job to set the table with a knife, fork and spoon at each place setting. How many pieces of silverware will you need to set the table? Show and tell how you know.

I have __14__ people coming to dinner.

I will need __20__ pieces of silverware.

I know because I counting by 3th

$3+3+3+3+3+1=14$

This response exhibits minimal awareness of the major elements. Only three place-mats are drawn. The answer, equation, and sentences are not valid.

Level Two

Your extended family is coming to your house for the holidays. It's your job to set the table with a knife, fork and spoon at each place setting. How many pieces of silverware will you need to set the table? Show and tell how you know.

I have ___6___ people coming to dinner.

I will need ___1⌐___ pieces of silverware.

I know because

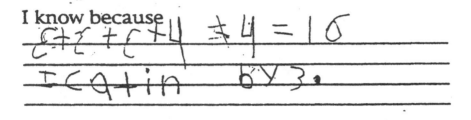

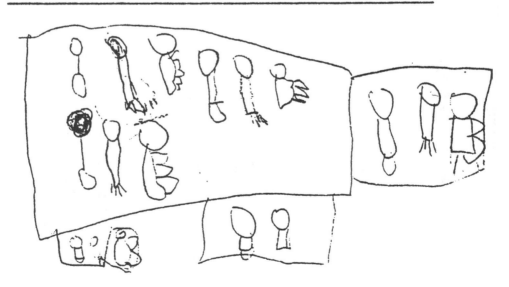

This response is mostly correct. The illustration supports the explanation but there's a piece missing on one of the place-mats, making the answer incorrect. The equation doesn't match the final conclusion.

Level Two

Your extended family is coming to your house for the holidays. It's your job to set the table with a knife, fork and spoon at each place setting. How many pieces of silverware will you need to set the table? Show and tell how you know.

I have _12_ people coming to dinner.

I will need _33_ pieces of silverware.

I know because _Their Weire 12 PeoPle._
ehey got a Knife.fork and a
sPoon.

$$3+3+3+3=12$$

This response shows the major elements: people around a table and three tallies to represent the silverware. However, one person did not get a set so the conclusion isn't accurate. The equation is correct, but it doesn't match the problem.

Level Three

Your extended family is coming to your house for the holidays. It's your job to set the table with a knife, fork and spoon at each place setting. How many pieces of silverware will you need to set the table? Show and tell how you know.

I have __6__ people coming to dinner.

I will need __18__ pieces of silverware.

I know because
There are 6 people coming and 18 silverware allooother;
3+3+3+3+3+3=18

This response reflects an appropriate strategy with all the elements accurately represented. The equation and sentence leads to a valid conclusion and complete understanding.

Level Four

Your extended family is coming to your house for the holidays. It's your job to set the table with a knife, fork and spoon at each place setting. How many pieces of silverware will you need to set the table? Show and tell how you know.

I have __15__ people coming to dinner.

I will need __45__ pieces of silverware.

I know because

I conted by 3's.
And I conted the
Silrweri

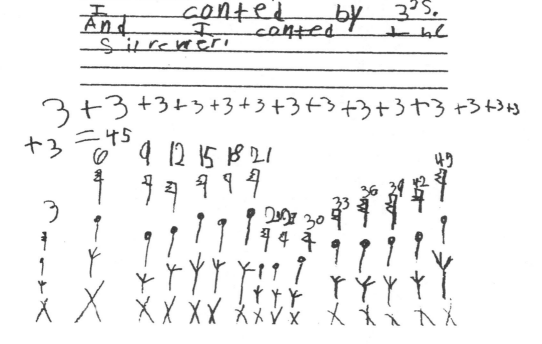

The student efficiently represented the 12 people with Xs and then drew a fork, spoon, and knife above each X. He counted by 3s and represented his strategy in an accurate equation and sentence.

Level Four

I have __18__ people coming to dinner.

I will need __54__ pieces of silverware.

I know because
_____ I couted by Threes
and I came up with 54.

I had alot of people in my
family to give knife, fork.
and a Spoon?

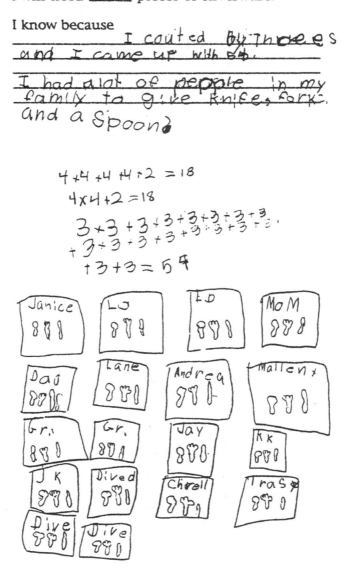

$4 + 4 + 4 + 4 + 2 = 18$

$4 \times 4 + 2 = 18$

$3 + 3 + 3 + 3 + 3 + 3 + 3 + 3$
$+ 3 + 3 + 3 + 3 + 3 + 3 + 3 =$
$+ 3 + 3 = 54$

Detailed illustration shows evidence of planning and complete understanding of the problem. Equations include addition and multiplication. Excellent synthesis of the task.

HOW MANY MORE?

Mathematics Assessed

- ◆ Counting and Cardinality
- ◆ Operations and Algebraic Thinking
- ◆ Habits of Mind
- ◆ Modeling and Using Tools.

Directions to the Student

- ◆ Your teacher will show you a frame (dot pattern or number card).
- ◆ Be ready to draw how many more you need to make 5, 10 or 20.
- ◆ Write an equation to show how you can make that combination.

(Note for teacher: The 10 frame provides a helpful structure, dot cards showing a scattered configurations would be more challenging, and number cards would be the most abstract. Adjust the task accordingly.)

Kindergarteners may be working within 5 and 10 (possibly with five frame and dot cards to five, first). First graders may be working within 10 and 20. Second graders may be working within 20 from memory (possibly with a double ten frame, first).

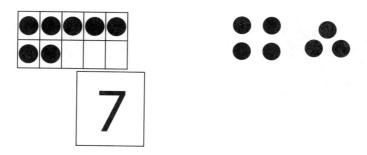

About This Task

In this task, students are asked to demonstrate computational fluency within 5, 10 and 20. They are quickly subitzing (instantly recognizing how many dots are present) and then thinking about how many more to make a landmark number of 5, 10 and 20. Begin with frames, scattered configurations/

dots, and finally to the symbolic representation of a numeral. This automaticity is essential for a procedural fluency with number combinations, creating mental images for doubles and structures of 5 and 10. Essentially, this is the "missing addend" problem to showcase the relationship between addition and subtraction.

Solution

Solutions will vary depending on your number range and materials (frames, dot cards and numerals-moving from the concrete to the abstract). Watch to see which students name the number/quantity automatically, use some composite grouping strategies, or begins counting all, or counting on.

Rubric

	Level One	Level Two	Level Three	Level Four
Problem Solving Approach	No organization for counting; some 1–1 correspondence.	Counts all or counts on from the number or quantity.	Uses grouping structures 2, 5, 10 or 20.	Uses visuals and symbolic representations; doubles or make ten facts.
Accuracy and Precision	Inaccurately counts all; little evidence of cardinality.	Automatically names the next number in a sequence; creates a mental image.	Uses a mental image and a variety of efficient strategies, accurately.	Knows from memory, how many more are needed.
Communication	Needs to see and touch the dots on the frame or card to explain how many.	Explains how many, how many more, using 1–1 counting or a mental image.	Explains how to count up, or use groups to make the total/sum flexibly.	Explains the inverse operation between addition and subtraction.

IS IT 15?

Mathematics Assessed

- ◆ Counting and Cardinality
- ◆ Operations and Algebraic Thinking
- ◆ Geometry
- ◆ Reasoning and Explaining
- ◆ Modeling and Using Tools.

Directions to the Student

- ◆ If the area of the green triangle is one, name the area of the other pattern blocks below.

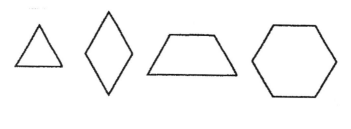

- ◆ Can you create two different designs with an area that equals exactly 15?
- ◆ How many pieces did you use on the first design? _____
- ◆ How many pieces did you use on the second? _____
- ◆ What else did you notice?

About This Task

This tasks asks students to create a composite shape from three pattern blocks, based on the proportional relationship and a pre-determined unit. They apply that understanding to build two-dimensional designs. Students can be challenged to come up with multiple solutions for this task.

Visual spatial skills can also be assessed during the construction process. Invite students to also share their computation methods with one another.

If symmetry and congruence are part of the standards for students, be sure to clarify the expectations in the directions to the students.

Solution

Given some time, students will create a variety of designs and solution strategies. At least one of their designs should have a total are of 15 and an equation that explains their computation strategy. This task can be split into several sessions and the total area could be reduced to 10 or less for younger students.

Rubric

	Level One	Level Two	Level Three	Level Four
Problem Solving Approach	Design project is unplanned and random; disorganized.	Design project is attempted with minimal organization.	Design project, answers, and reproduction are organized.	Design project is complete and well-planned.
Accuracy and Precision	Computation is inaccurate; major errors design, area, and equation.	Computation is mostly accurate; designs have an area close to 15 units.	Computation is accurate; area and a correct equation.	Computation is accurate; an efficient use of a formula or computation strategy is demonstrated.
Communication	Explanation shows a limited understanding of the concepts.	Explanation represents only some parts of the process.	Explanation demonstrates a complete understanding of area.	Explanation includes a synthesis of the area concept including precise mathematical language.

Samples of Student Work

Level One

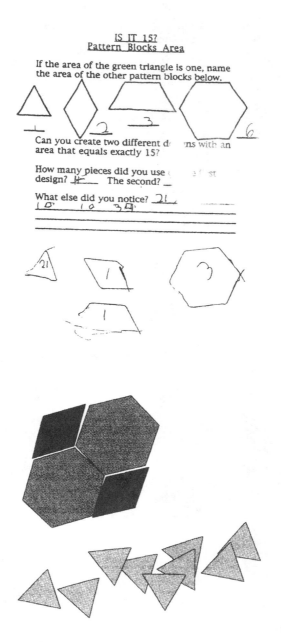

This response had major errors with area. It shows a limited understanding of the problem posed in this task.

Level Two

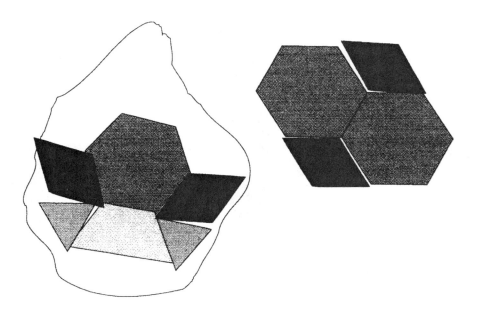

IS IT 15?
Pattern Blocks Area

If the area of the green triangle is one, name
the area of the other pattern blocks below.

_1_ _2_ _3_ _6_

Can you create two different designs with an
area that equals exactly 15?

How many pieces did you use on the first
design? _6_   The second? _5_

What else did you notice? *That   It*
look like a robot   with
no hdo.   It look+ like
an eagle.

This response shows a partial understanding of area. The first design has an
area of 15, but the second has an area of 16. His remarks about the first design
read, *"That it looked like a robot with no head,"* and the second design, *"It looked
like an eagle."*

Level Three

IS IT 15?
Pattern Blocks Area

If the area of the green triangle is one, name
the area of the other pattern blocks below.

<u>1</u>   <u>2</u>   <u>3</u>   <u>6</u>

Can you create two different designs with an
area that equals exactly 15?

How many pieces did you use on the first
design? __5__   The second? __6__

What else did you notice? _I___notice_
_that__one__of__my__patterns_looks_
_like__a__UFO.__I__notice_
_that__both__of__my__patterns_Have_Sammit
                                              y.

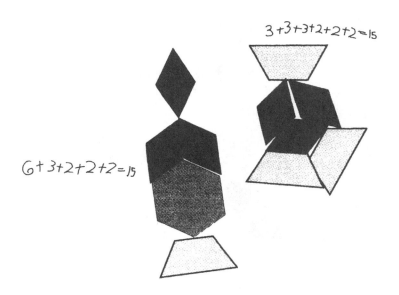

$$3+3+3+2+2+2=15$$

$$6+3+2+2+2=15$$

This response met the area requirements and included correct equations.

Level Four

<u>IS IT 15?</u>
<u>Pattern Blocks Area</u>

If the area of the green triangle is one, name
the area of the other pattern blocks below.

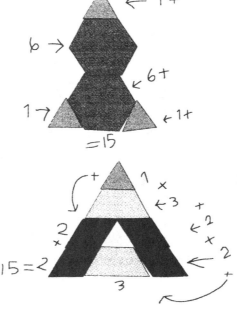

Can you create two different designs with an
area that equals exactly 15?

How many pieces did you use on the first
design? _7_   The second? _5_

What else did you notice? _all tagthr in my_
designs their are 30

This response is clear, complete, and accurate. The explanation shows a synthesis of the task, an understanding of area, and an interesting observation about the combined area of both designs.

LOSING TEETH

Mathematics Assessed

- ◆ Operations and Algebraic Thinking
- ◆ Number Operations and Base Ten
- ◆ Measurement and Data
- ◆ Reasoning and Explaining
- ◆ Modeling and Using Tools.

Directions to the Student

Ask at least nine students in your class how many teeth they have lost. Record your lost teeth, too.

How many teeth is that all together? _____

Make a graph to show your results and then answer these questions.

Who lost the most teeth? _____
Who lost the fewest teeth? _____
What else did you notice about the data? _____

To complete this task you should:

- ◆ Collect the information.
- ◆ Represent the number of teeth lost by each member of your group with a white paper square and make a graph.
- ◆ Answer the questions and write at least one statement about what you noticed.

About This Task

This task requires students to collect and organize data from at least nine students in their class, including themselves. They create a pictograph or diagram using one square centimeter or inch paper units. Then they compare and interpret the data and record at least one observation statement about the results.

Solution

Solutions will vary depending on the group size and the age of the students in the class. Most samples will not have the same distributions of teeth, which can also be an interesting conversation. Teachers may want to post the displays and compare and contrast the information.

Rubric

	Level One	Level Two	Level Three	Level Four
Problem Solving Approach	Information is disorganized or incomplete.	Information is mostly complete and transferable data; < 9 people.	Information is organized into a visual representation; data collected; = or > 9 people.	Information is organized in an efficient way; may include > 9 people.
Accuracy and Precision	Major computation errors lead to inaccurate work.	Minor computation errors lead to reasonable, but incorrect displays and comparisons.	Correct calculations lead to correct displays and comparisons.	Correct calculations lead to well- developed comparisons and an accurate synthesis of the data.
Communication	Explanation is missing or unclear.	Explanation is incomplete or inaccurate.	Explanation has valid conclusions; supported by the data.	Explanation includes making connections between the age, group size, and data.

MEASURE ME

Mathematics Assessed

◆ Counting and Cardinality
◆ Measurement and Data
◆ Habits of Mind
◆ Modeling and Using Tools.

Directions to the Student

Have a friend trace your body on a large piece of paper. You can be a friend and trace their body, too! How many ways can we measure you? Choose a linear measurement unit and predict and measure at least five lengths. Record your guess and final check. Have your partner check your work.

About This Task

This task requires students to apply skills in measurement and calculation to a practical situation. The students need to measure, to a reasonable degree of accuracy, at least five linear dimensions and record their results. Provide optional standard and nonstandard units for measurement such as unifix cubes, tiles, toothpicks, learning links, rulers, tape measures, and yardsticks.

Young children need a variety of experiences iterating units (putting them side-by-side without any gaps or overlaps). Non-standard units provide an opportunity for this practice, which develops an understanding of grouped units like inches on a ruler.

Generally, kindergarten and first grade students are assessed with non-standard units, and second graders are assessed with standard units including inches, feet, centimeters and meters. First and second graders should also have experiences with measuring the same distance with two different sized units. For example, a craft stick and a linking cube. Understanding that the size of the unit relates to the number of units one needs is a big idea! Fewer craft sticks are needed because they are longer.

Solution

Solutions will vary depending on the size and age of your group of students. The steps in the process should be modeled frequently. Experiences with multiple measurement instruments are critical for a child's understanding.

Rubric

	Level One	Level Two	Level Three	Level Four
Problem Solving Approach	The approach to the work is disorganized; unfinished.	The approach to the work is evident but incomplete.	The approach and display is complete.	The approach and display shows advanced planning; record-keeping is organized.
Accuracy and Precision	The solution has major errors in estimation and actual measurement.	The solution has minor errors in estimation and actual measurement.	The solution has minor errors in the estimates and accurate measurements.	The solution has reasonable estimates and accurate measurements.
Communication	The explanation shows confusion about measurement concepts and tools.	The explanation shows an understanding of "how to" measure something.	The explanation shows an understanding of linear measurement tools and units.	The explanation shows a clear understanding of measurement tools and units in relationship to one another.

NUMBER LINE

Mathematics Assessed

- ◆ Counting and Cardinality
- ◆ Number Operations and Base Ten
- ◆ Habits of Mind
- ◆ Modeling and Using Tools.

Directions to the Student

Kindergarten

- ◆ Label the end points on your number line 0 and 10.
- ◆ Count by ones to 10 and label those numbers.
- ◆ If you were to extend your number line, what would come after 10?
- ◆ Show your thinking.
- ◆ What do you notice?

First Grade

- ◆ Label the end points on your number line 0 and 120.
- ◆ Count by tens to 120 and label those numbers.
- ◆ Label these numbers on the number line: 25, 41, and 67.
- ◆ How did you know where those numbers go?
- ◆ Now label 10 more than 25, 41, and 67.
- ◆ What do you notice?

Second Grade

- ◆ Label the end points on your number line 0 and 1,000.
- ◆ Count by hundreds to 1,000 and label those numbers.
- ◆ Label these numbers on the number line: 120, 350 and 867.
- ◆ How did you know where those numbers go?
- ◆ Now label 100 more than 120, 350 and 867.
- ◆ What do you notice?

About This Task

The linear characteristic of the number line is well suited for exploring proportional reasoning. This model invites students to partition or subdivide the space or distance, based on place value and number relationships. Students might initially use the number line for counting by 1s, then 10s and 100s. Later, this model can be used to find the difference between two numbers or a measurement tool for fraction understanding. In this task, students construct their own number line and then demonstrate their mental math skills adding and subtracting 10s and 100s.

Solution

Solutions will vary depending on the prompts for each grade level. Begin by looking for the mid-point or landmark number. For example, half of 10 is 5. Is the 5 in the middle of the line? Are the marks fairly equally spaced and are the numbers in order? Can the student name the number before and after any given number on the line? Can the student mentally count on 10 more or less than any given number? A 100 more/less?

Rubric

	Level One	Level Two	Level Three	Level Four
Problem Solving Approach	Approach is not evident; no attention to mid-point; numbers are out of order.	Approach located mid-point; numbers are in order, but not to scale.	Approach is planned and shows some spatial relationships.	Approach is well planned using landmark numbers; shows numbers in order, and to scale.
Accuracy and Precision	Inaccurately labeled numbers.	Minor errors in labeling the mid-point and numbers.	Accurately labeled z; shows number sense.	Accurately shows proportional relationships.
Communication	Explanation shows a limited understanding of how to use a number line.	Explanation shows a fragile understanding of how to use a number line.	Explanation shows an understanding of a number line as a model.	Explanation uses a number line to model place value language and relational thinking.

Samples of Student Work

These student work samples are from a second grade classroom, working within 1,000, mentally adding hundreds to any given number.

Level One

This student places numbers on the line, with little attention to the order. For example, 867 comes before 500. Five hundred, the mid-point of this number line was originally in the middle but then erased and placed off center. Some numbers are also missing; 100, 200, 300, 400, 220, 450, and 967.

Level Two

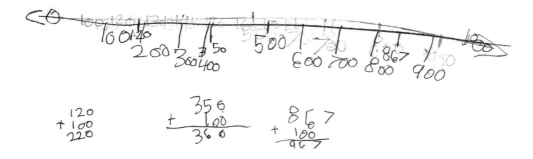

$$\begin{array}{r} 120 \\ + 100 \\ \hline 220 \end{array}$$

$$\begin{array}{r} 350 \\ + 100 \\ \hline 350 \end{array}$$

$$\begin{array}{r} 867 \\ + 100 \\ \hline 967 \end{array}$$

This student labeled the mid-point in the middle of the line, after several attempts. The number 120 is located between 100 and 200, but incorrectly labeled closer to the 200; 350 is located after 400; 867 is labeled between 800 and 900 but closer to 800, rather than 900. This child was not able to mentally add 100 to any given number and was dependent on paper-pencil computation.

Level Three

This student accurately identified the mid-point, and labeled the 100s in relationship to each other. He was able to explain that 120 is more than 100 and less than 200, but the placement doesn't reflect an understanding that 120 is closer to 100, than 200. That said, 350 and 450 were centered between 300 and 400, and 867 and 967 were placed closer to the next hundred. Often students are "learning on the job" while performing a task.

Level Four

120 350
867
220 967
450

This student recorded the additional numbers on top of the paper and then explained how he "just knew" that 100 more would be 220, 450 and 967. He revised his placement a few times to accurate represent the given number as closer to or farther away from the hundred landmarks and used 50 as a benchmark number.

NUMBER TREES

Mathematics Assessed

- ◆ Counting and Cardinality
- ◆ Operations and Algebraic Thinking
- ◆ Number Operations and Base Ten
- ◆ Habits of Mind
- ◆ Reasoning and Explaining.

Directions to the Student

- ◆ Fold the paper to make 6–8 boxes.
- ◆ Draw a picture and/or a number tree to show how you could decompose a number.
- ◆ Write an expression or equation in each box.
- ◆ Be ready to explain your thinking to the class.

About This Task

Encourage your kindergarten students to begin with concrete models, then move to representing the quantities with a picture. Moving from the concrete, to the abstract, writing equations and expressions, is fundamental to early numeracy development. Begin with decomposing 5, then 10, and then numbers in the range of 11–20. First graders should comfortably record number trees for numbers from 11 to 120 by the end of the year. Their work should reflect the commutative property and 10s and 1s thinking with place value. Second graders might begin with 100 and work up to 1,000 by the end of the year. Understanding and applying the idea of equivalence and the meaning of the equal sign, is another key concept. Example:

$$5 + 6 = 10 + 1$$

Some teachers like to practice this idea with the date on the calendar, or the number of school days, markers and white boards. Then the task becomes an extension of the teaching sequence.

Solution

Teachers might consider offering a choice of numbers within a range to differentiate the assessment task. Look for evidence of patterns and structure showing one more and one less, the application of the commutative property and the use of the zero property for addition. Sharing student work as a community provides a forum for comparing and contrasting student strategies.

Rubric

	Level One	Level Two	Level Three	Level Four
Problem Solving Approach	Information is incomplete and lacks planning; contains few examples, expressions, and equations.	Information is complete and shows some attempt at planning but is difficult to follow.	Information is complete, planned out, and organized.	Information shows a clear plan; demonstrates place value and properties reasoning.
Accuracy and Precision	Incorrect or missing expressions and equations.	Minor errors in expressions or equations.	Accurate equations or expressions.	Accurate and challenging equations or expressions.
Communication	Explanation is unclear or confused.	Explanation includes at least two strategies.	Explanation includes a variety of strategies; doubles, make ten, and fact families.	Explanation shows flexible, efficient and accurate ways of reasoning; computational fluency.

Samples of Student Work

These student work samples are from a kindergarten and first grade classroom, working within 10 and the teen numbers.

Level Three

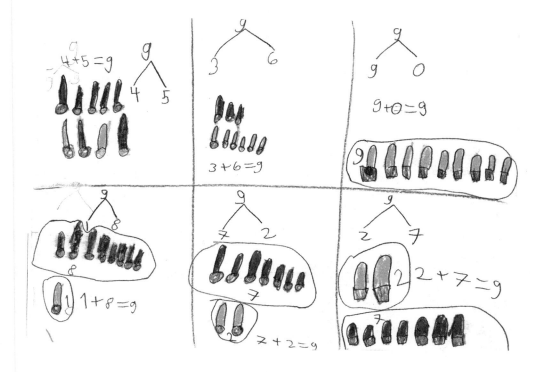

This kindergarten student decomposes the number 9 and draws a picture in two colors, to show the two addends. She shows evidence of the commutative property by using fact families. She also includes an example of the zero property for addition.

Level Three

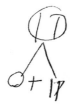

In the first month of first grade, this student, decomposed the number 11. She no longer needed to draw a picture and wrote the expression. Her work follows a pattern of one more and one less. During her presentation to the class you said, "She knew 5 + 6 = 11 because 5 + 5 would be 10, and 1 more would be 11." Young children are often able to tell more than they can show in a written record.

PAPER QUILTS

Mathematics Assessed

- ◆ Counting and Cardinality
- ◆ Operations and Algebraic Thinking
- ◆ Geometry
- ◆ Modeling and Using Tools
- ◆ Seeing Structure and Generalizing.

Directions to the Student

You will each construct a star quilt pattern for a class quilt project. Decide which two colors of construction paper squares you will use to represent the two fields of color. Glue the pieces onto the paper pattern provided according to your key. You will want to cut your square pieces into triangles so that they will fit your quilt block pattern. Cut out the finished quilt square.

Answer these questions:

- ◆ How many triangles of color #1 did you use?
- ◆ How many triangles of color #2 did you use?
- ◆ How many triangles of both colors did you use all together?
- ◆ What is the square area of this quilt block?
- ◆ What else did you notice? Can you think of three other things?

Quilt Squares

Evening Star

name _____

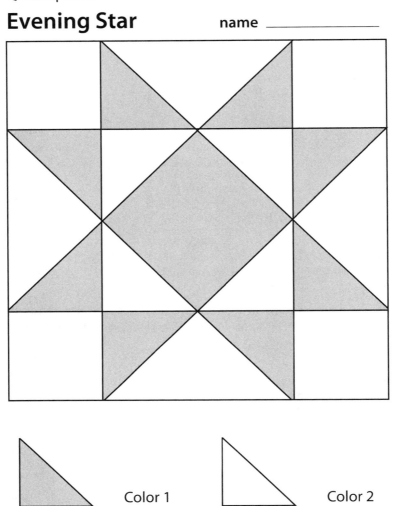

Color 1   Color 2

About This Task

This task requires students to apply a key to a quilt design. Students apply spatial reasoning to rotate triangles to fit into the template. Much like puzzles, this requires problem solving and geometric thinking.

Solution

There are two possible solutions to this activity if you only use two colors. Students may notice patterns, diagonal, vertical, and horizontal lines, angles, and so forth. Multiple opportunities exist with more than two color combinations and more complex quilt designs. This activity lends itself to sorting the completed quilt blocks, to building a class quilt with all the individual pieces, and to a lesson on area, perimeter, and factoring with older students.

Rubric

	Level One	**Level Two**	**Level Three**	**Level Four**
Problem Solving Approach	Information doesn't match the key or is unorganized.	Information matches the key; difficulty with layout.	Information and layout match the key.	Information shows planning, in the approach and layout
Accuracy and Precision	Incorrect quilt model and responses to questions.	Mostly correct quilt model and responses to questions.	Correct quilt model and responses to questions.	Quilt model is complete and responses to the questions go beyond the obvious.
Communication	Presentation shows no evidence of geometry or number concepts.	Presentation includes less than 3 statements that correctly reflect geometry or number concepts.	Presentation includes 3 statements that reflect geometry or number concepts.	Presentation includes 3 or more statements that include precise mathematical vocabulary.

PIZZA NIGHT

Mathematics Assessed

- ◆ Counting and Cardinality
- ◆ Operations and Algebraic Thinking
- ◆ Number Operations and Base Ten
- ◆ Reasoning and Explaining
- ◆ Modeling and Using Tools.

Directions to the Student

You and your family have ordered one extra-large pizza for supper. The pizza is cut into 18 slices. How many slices will you get if everyone gets the same amount? Show and tell your work.

There are _____ members in my family.

Each person will get _____ slices of pizza.

About This Task

In this task, students are asked to illustrate their thinking and to write an equation and a few sentences about how they thought about the problem. Students whose families contain 2, 3, 6, or 9 members will have an easier job, since those numbers are factors of 18, and they won't have to calculate fractions. Students can organize the information in a graphic format and demonstrate what they know about dividing up equal shares and fractions. Young students may need additional manipulative support and may be interviewed in lieu of the written assignment.

Solution

Solutions will vary depending on the number of family members: 2 members will share 9 pieces each, 3 members will share 6 pieces, 4 members will share 4½ pieces, 5 members will share 3⅗ pieces, 6 members will share 3 pieces,

7 members will share $2\frac{4}{7}$ pieces, and 8 members will share $2\frac{1}{4}$ pieces. Students may want to justify giving the adults more, a real life adaptation, rather than work with the abstract fractions.

Rubric

	Level One	Level Two	Level Three	Level Four
Problem Solving Approach	Information is random and difficult to follow.	Information is mostly complete; visual display is disorganized.	Information is complete; the visual display reflects some of the problem.	Information is clearly identified and the visual display reflects the complete problem.
Accuracy and Precision	The omissions and major errors lead to invalid results.	The minor errors may lead to an error.	There are no errors; the computation and understanding of mathematical concepts are correct.	There are no errors; the application of number concepts, notation, and conclusions are above grade level.
Communication	The explanation shows serious gaps in understanding; inaccurate conclusions.	The explanation shows an incomplete understanding of equal shares or division.	The explanation communicates an appropriate division strategy and understanding of equal shares.	The explanation includes precise mathematical vocabulary.

Samples of Student Work

Level One

You and your family have ordered one extra-large pizza for supper. The pizza is cut into 18 pieces. How many pieces will you get if everyone gets the same amount? Show and tell your work.

There are __4__ members in my family.

I will get __5x__ pieces of pizza.

MY F B   G 4 PIzz.   I like a 10000
                              p izza.

8 ÷ 5 = 00

This response is random and difficult to follow. The statements and equations do not match the conclusion to this problem.

Level Two

You and your family have ordered one extra-large pizza for
supper. The pizza is cut into 18 pieces. How many pieces will
you get if everyone gets the same amount? Show and tell
your work.
There are ____4____ members in my family.
I will get ____4____ pieces of pizza.

This response shows the pizza, the four members of the family, and the
beginnings of understanding division. "I had 4 in a hafa so did my famay."
However, the equation doesn't match the illustration or explanation.

Level Two

You and your family have ordered one extra-large pizza for supper. The pizza is cut into 18 pieces. How many pieces will you get if everyone gets the same amount? Show and tell your work.

There are __6__ members in my family.

I will get __2__ pieces of pizza.

6 lift ovr and My family

I cotid by 2s

This response is an example of a minor flaw that leads to an inaccurate conclusion. The student did not follow through with the remaining pieces. There is a clear graphic display, the sentence supports the conclusion, and there is evidence of counting by 2s. So close!

Level Three

You and your family have ordered one extra-large pizza for supper. The pizza is cut into 18 pieces. How many pieces will you get if everyone gets the same amount? Show and tell your work.

There are __4__ members in my family.

I will get __4__ pieces of pizza.

I would get 4 becuse 4+4+5+'5 =
18 I conted by 4's. be 6 but it
I thoght it would
is th
←mom is over there

Domahoes

dad

I desited the klds shⅽed get 4
a the adalts sheedged 5,

This response displays all the elements of the problem. The conclusion, *"I decided the kids should get 4 and the adults should get 5"* is a real-life explanation for the remainder.

Level Four

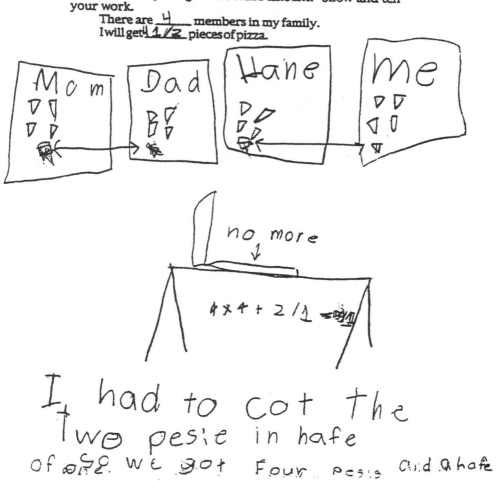

You and your family have ordered one extra-large pizza for supper. The pizza is cut into 18 pieces. How many pieces will you get if everyone gets the same amount? Show and tell your work.

There are ___4___ members in my family.
I will get _1 1/2_ pieces of pizza.

Mom

Dad

Hane

me

no more

4 x 4 + 2/1

I had to cot the two pesie in hafe of one. we got four pesis and a hafe

This response clearly demonstrates the student's understanding of division and fractions. The student writes, *"I had to cut the two pieces in half, so we got four pieces and a half of one."*

Level Four

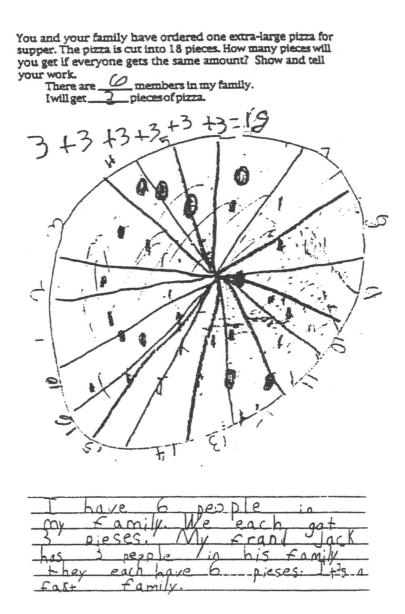

You and your family have ordered one extra-large pizza for supper. The pizza is cut into 18 pieces. How many pieces will you get if everyone gets the same amount? Show and tell your work.

There are __6__ members in my family.
I will get __3__ pieces of pizza.

$3 + 3 + 3 + 3 + 3 + 3 = 18$

I have 6 people in my family. We each got 3 pieses. My frand Jack has 3 people in his family they each have 6 pieses. It's a fast family.

This response identifies all the elements of the problem. This student was working next to another student who had three people in his family. As the two were thinking out loud and counting, he noticed the relationship between the two answers (3 × 6, 6 × 3). *"It's a fact family"* was his explanation for the communicative property of multiplication.

THE SAME SIZE AS ME

Mathematics Assessed

- ◆ Counting and Cardinality
- ◆ Measurement and Data
- ◆ Habits of Mind
- ◆ Modeling and Using Tools.

Directions to the Student

Use cotton string to measure the circumference (that is, the distance around) your head. Measure right across your ears and forehead. Have a friend check your work. Record your results. Compare your measurement with your partner's. Whose circumference is longer? Are they the same? Record your results.

Find someone else in the room who measures the same as you. Record your results.

Look around the classroom. Use your string. Can you find five people or things that measure the same as you? Record your results.

About This Task

This task requires students to use tools to measure their head circumference and to help a partner measure his or hers. Students also compare their results to other students, their classroom environment, and their own body. Estimation and recordkeeping are also being assessed.

Metric and U.S. Customary units can be used for practice with standard units of measurements. Cotton string or cord is best to avoid "stretching" in materials like yarn.

Solution

Solutions will vary depending on the size and age of your class. Comparison words like "longer, longest, short and shortest" would be appropriate for kindergarten students. First graders should use non-standard units to measure the string. Second graders should use standard units with labels. The vocabulary and process should be modeled frequently with thematic applications to pumpkins, snowmen, animals, globes, gym balls, and so forth.

Rubric

	Level One	Level Two	Level Three	Level Four
Problem Solving Approach	Information is incomplete and disorganized.	Information is mostly complete with an attempt to organize data.	Information is complete and data is organized.	Information shows evidence of planning; data is clear, concise, and organized.
Accuracy and Precision	Measurements are inaccurate.	Measurements are + or − 2 inches or four centimeters.	Measurements are accurate, + or − ½ inch or one centimeter.	Measurements are accurate and show evidence of efficient strategies.
Communication	Explanation is unclear.	Explanation shows an understanding of measuring; "what to do."	Explanation shows an understanding of the skills and tools necessary to measure something.	Explanation shows an understanding of measurement concepts, tools, and use of precise mathematical vocabulary.

SHAPES IN MY WORLD

Mathematics Assessed

- ◆ Geometry
- ◆ Modeling and Using Tools
- ◆ Seeing Structure and Generalizing.

Directions to the Student

- ◆ You'll be looking for the following shapes: (teachers will choose the appropriate shapes for their students).
- ◆ Identify the two- or three-dimensional shapes you'll be looking for:
- ◆ Can you find at least three examples of each of those shapes in your classroom or outdoor area?
- ◆ Record your ideas in pictures and/or writing.
- ◆ Share with your friends.

About This Task

This task encourages students to look in their real world environments in school, at home, and outdoors, for common two- and three-dimensional shapes. This task can be modified for each grade level depending on the curriculum objectives. Check your district requirements.

- ◆ Kindergarten: squares, circles, triangles, rectangles, hexagons, cubes, cones, cylinders, and spheres.
- ◆ First grade: rectangles, squares, trapezoids, triangles, half-circles, and quarter-circles, cubes, right rectangular prisms, right circular cones, and right circularcylinders.
- ◆ Second grade: triangles, quadrilaterals, pentagons, hexagons, and cubes.

Young children may feel more comfortable drawing pictures of the objects and labeling them. A ball may be represented as "BL." A round circle placed by the letters may help you read the work and stimulate the child's memory about the shape. The pictures provide support for their writing and presentation.

Patterns and relationships in nature can provide a rich setting for this task. This task can be repeated several different times during the year to assess student growth and progress.

Solution

Solutions will vary depending on the required shapes and the environment. Students will identify, categorize, and describe common geometric figures and draw conclusions about the relationship of shapes in their world.

Rubric

	Level One	**Level Two**	**Level Three**	**Level Four**
Problem Solving Approach	Record-keeping is unplanned, incomplete, or disorganized.	Record-keeping is complete but not organized.	Record-keeping is complete and organized.	Record-keeping is well planned and systematic.
Accuracy and Precision	Major errors in the pictures, labeling and/or writing.	Minor errors in the pictures, labeling and/or writing; < 3 examples.	No errors in the pictures, labeling, and/or writing; 3 examples each.	No errors; a variety of unique examples are chosen; or more than 3 examples of each.
Communication	The explanation shows no understanding of dimensions or attributes of shapes.	The explanation shows a partial understanding of dimensions and attributes of shapes.	The explanation shows an understanding of dimensions and attributes of shapes.	The explanation includes precise math vocabulary about the dimensions and attributes of shapes.

STORY PROBLEMS

Mathematics Assessed

- ◆ Operations and Algebraic Thinking
- ◆ Number Operations and Base Ten
- ◆ Habits of Mind
- ◆ Reasoning and Explaining.

Directions to the Student

Today, each of you will create a story problem. You will use the storyboards and counters provided to make your story. Your story must match your storyboard picture. Think of a mathematical question you could ask about your picture. Write an equation that reflects your math question. Include the answer.

Be ready to present your story problem to the class.

About This Task

The children will need time to explore with the materials they will be using. Allow students time to share their own initial stories orally with a partner. Teachers can model sample story problems for practice. Students will solve them on their own storyboard while the teacher repeats the problem. The children will share their solutions with each other. After this introductory lesson, children will be ready to create their own storyboards. Students can write their own stories or dictate them to an adult.

When the students share their stories with the class, other students will want to solve the posed problem using manipulative, pictures, numbers, or words. Many approaches are valued. Teachers can evaluate the project at the time of student oral presentation.

Solution

Answers will vary according to the story problems the students pose. Teachers should pose more challenging missing addend or subtrahend, comparing, multiplication, and division problems, so that the students can authentically demonstrate their understanding of mathematics through creative, inventive, problem solving solutions.

Teachers can introduce one given number for a whole group lesson and challenge students to come up with a representation of that quantity in addition or subtraction stories. This story-telling lesson allows students to see the relationship between addition and subtraction operations ($7 + 1 = 8$ and $8 - 1 = 7$). Encourage students to represent subtraction in other than removal methods, as in missing addend and comparing models.

Student stories might reflect the number quantity and operation in the grade-level instruction goals. For example:

Kindergarten student may be working within 5 the first half of the year, progressing to story problems within 10.

First graders may be working within 10 the first half of the year, progressing to story problems within 20.

Second graders may be working within 20 the first half of the year, progressing to story problems within 100. Some students may also be interested in multiplication as repeated addition word problems.

Rubric

	Level One	Level Two	Level Three	Level Four
Problem Solving Approach	Story or picture is incomplete and lacks evidence of planning.	Story doesn't match picture and shows only some evidence of planning.	Story matches picture; all the information is planned and complete.	Story matches picture; evidence of planning and a clear organizational system
Posing a Question	Question is missing; may make a statement.	Question is incompatible; doesn't match picture.	Question involves simple computation (How many all together? How many are left?)	Question is higher level (fewer than; greater than) or contains multiple steps.
Written Equation	Equation is missing.	Equation or solution is incorrect.	Equation and solution are correct.	Equation is challenging and is written using age appropriate notation.
Communication	Presentation is incomplete and inaccurate.	Presentation is incomplete or incorrect; student is unable to self-correct the errors.	Presentation is correct and shows an understanding of problem solving.	Presentation shows an understanding of complex problem solving; with precise mathematical vocabulary.

Samples of Student Work

Level Two

It was snowing and there were
10 snowmen and 6 more went sliding
and 4 mittens stad home with the
other 10 how mene stad home?

This response doesn't match the picture or have a completed equation or an answer.

Level Three

Once upon a time there were sthree snowmen sleding and there were four mittens on the line drying and santa man was flying in his sled How many snowmen all togethr 3+3=? [6]

This response has a story that matches the picture, a math question, equation and correct answer with notation. One of the snowmen is "Santaman." The student also included unnecessary information in the story problem.

Level Four

Once upon a time there were
12. 4 snowmen went sledding at
Lions park. The rest stayed home
and drunk hot choklit. How
many drunk hot choklit? 12—4=8

This response shows evidence of planning. The student poses a missing addend question using a secret door. It has a correct sentence and answer.

| WORD PROBLEM TYPES: ON THE FARM |

Mathematics Assessed

- ◆ Operations and Algebraic Thinking
- ◆ Number Operations and Base Ten
- ◆ Reasoning and Explaining
- ◆ Modeling and Using Tools.

(Note: See the Appendix at the end of this chapter for the table that appears on page 88 of the Common Core State Standards for Mathematics document, which identifies the problem types that students are responsible for in K-2.)

Directions to the Student

Today, you'll solve a word problem about a situation that happened on a farm or ranch. Illustrate the situation and write and equation to show how you solved it. Be ready to present your work to the class.

(Note: The word problems are provided as student handouts on our website, www.routledge.com/9781138906891, to target the word problem types identified by the CCSS.)

About This Task

Depending on the grade level and time of year, teachers can adjust which problem types are practiced and assessed, and how large the number combinations are. Students can use objects, then pictures. Simple tallies or circles to illustrate the situation are fine. Extra credit should not be given for a cute illustration.

In some cases students may solve a missing addend prompt with subtraction, or a subtraction prompt by thinking about a missing addend. This ability to understand and apply the inverse operation is essential for computational fluency.

This task will assess an understanding of the unknown in all three positions. Some students may begin to use a letter or symbol for the unknown. Example: $4 + \_\_\_ = 6$

Solution

Solutions will vary depending on the number combinations and problem types. Several first grade work samples are provided for the following prompts:

Take from/result unknown: The farmer had 6 chicks, but he can only find 4. How many are missing? 6 − 4 = _____

Rubric

	Level One	Level Two	Level Three	Level Four
Problem Solving Approach	Information is incomplete or impossible to follow.	Information is complete, but difficult to follow.	Information is complete and organized.	Information is well organized to show an understanding of the problem type.
Accuracy and Precision	Inaccurate illustration and equation.	Accurate illustration or equation, but not both.	Accurate illustration and equation.	Accurate illustration and equation; challenging problem type.
Communication	Explanation is missing or incomplete.	Explanation shows a partial understanding of the problem solving.	Explanation shows a complete understanding of the problem.	Explanation may include multiple operations and solution strategies.

Samples of Student Work

Level One

Put together/take apart addend unknown: I see 8 horses in the field. Three are brown and the rest are black. How many are black? $8 - 3 = ?$ or $3 + \_\_ = 8$.

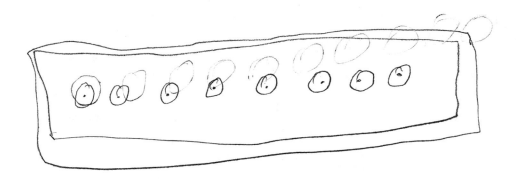

When the addend is unknown, students sometimes struggle and revert to solving for the total. In this student work you see the illustration for 8 horses, but no evidence of labeling 3 brown horses and how that might help find the number of black horses. The student also wrote an incorrect equation for adding $8 + 3$.

Level Two

Comparison/difference unknown: Ken had 9 goats and Kait had 7. How many more goats does Ken have than Kait? $9 - 7 =$ _____ or $7 +$ ___ $= 9$

Ken has two more

This student set up a comparison clearly. He labeled the 9 goats Ken had and, underneath, illustrated the goats that Kait had to find the difference of 2. He did write his answer in word form, but forgot the equation. During his presentation time, other students asked him where the equation was, and he was able to add it, $9 - 7 = 2$. When teachers make time for presentations, students have a chance to edit their work, and the assessment task reflects what the child can really do. Based on the work you see, the child would score at a Level 2. Based on what the child presented, the score would be a Level 3.

Level Three

The farmer had 6 chicks, but he can only find 4. How many are missing?

The student illustrates 6 cute chicks, crosses out 2 and then confirms that 6 − 2 = 4. The problem could also be solved as 6 − 4 = 2 and the child commented on that during the presentation to the class.

Level Three

Add to/change unknown: 4 robins were looking for worms. A few more joined them and now there are 7. How many robins came to join the robins?
4 + ____ = 7

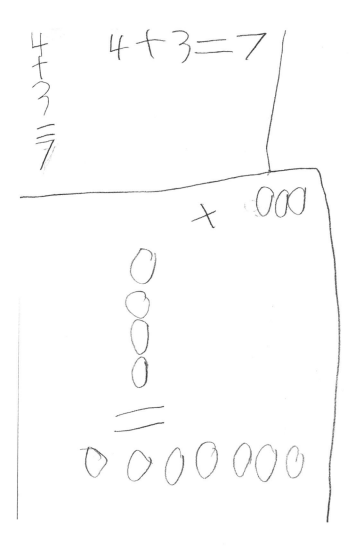

This student solved the prompt with the picture first, and then moved to the abstract/symbolic equation. Note the confusion about the equal sign, when the equation is written vertically. This is fairly typical in first grade classrooms.

Level Three

Put together/take apart total unknown: 2 cats and 7 dogs were playing on the grass. How many pets were playing on the grass? $2 + 7 =$ _____

$$2 + 7 = 9$$

7 dogs

OOCOOOO

oo 2 cats

This student drew and labeled the dogs and cats and counted on from 7 to solve the prompt. These "how many all together?" prompts are generally easier for students to put together using a counting all or counting on strategy.

Appendix

Table 1 Common addition and Subtraction situations.[6]

	Result Unknown	Change Unknown	Start Unknown
Add to	Two bunnies sat on the grass. Three more bunnies hopped there. How many bunnies are on the grass now? $2 + 3 = ?$	Two bunnies were sitting on the grass. Some more bunnies hopped there. Then there were five bunnies. How many bunnies hopped over to the first two? $2 + ? = 5$	Some bunnies were sitting on the grass. Three more bunnies hopped there. Then there were five bunnies. How many bunnies were on the grass before? $? + 3 = 5$
Take from	Five apples were on the table. I ate two apples. How many apples are on the table now? $5 - 2 = ?$	Five apples were on the table. I ate some apples. Then there were three apples. How many apples did I eat? $5 - ? = 3$	Some apples were on the table. I ate two apples. Then there were three apples. How many apples were on the table before? $? - 2 = 3$

	Total Unknown	Addend Unknown	Both Addends Unknown[1]
Put Together/Take Apart[2]	Three red apples and two green apples are on the table. How many apples are on the table? $3 + 2 = ?$	Five apples are on the table. Three are red and the rest are green. How many apples are green? $3 + ? = 5, 5 - 3 = ?$	Grandma has five flowers. How many can she put in her red vase and how many in her blue vase? $5 = 0 + 5, 5 = 5 + 0$ $5 = 1 + 4, 5 = 4 + 1$ $5 = 2 + 3, 5 = 3 + 2$

	Difference Unknown	Bigger Unknown	Smaller Unknown
Compare[3]	("How many more?" version): Lucy has two apples. Julie has five apples. How many more apples does Julie have than Lucy? ("How many fewer?" version): Lucy has two apples. Julie has five apples. How many fewer apples does Lucy have than Julie? $2 + ? = 5, 5 - 2 = ?$	(Version with "more"): Julie has three more apples than Lucy. Lucy has two apples. How many apples does Julie have? (Version with "fewer"): Lucy has 3 fewer apples than Julie. Lucy has two apples. How many apples does Julie have? $2 + 3 = ?, 3 + 2 = ?$	(Version with "more"): Julie has three more apples than Lucy. Julie has five apples. How many apples does Lucy have? (Version with "fewer"): Lucy has 3 fewer apples than Julie. Julie has five apples. How many apples does Lucy have? $5 - 3 = ?, ? + 3 = 5$

Source: *Common Core State Standards for Mathematics.*